THE ALL-NEW

CLEAN
JOKE
BOOK

BOB PHILLIPS

HARVEST HOUSE PUBLISHERS
Eugene, Oregon 97402

To Lisa, Christy, Jon-Mark, and Ryan
who are as crazy as some of these jokes.

THE ALL-NEW CLEAN JOKE BOOK

Copyright © 1990 by Harvest House Publishers
Eugene, Oregon 97402

Phillips, Bob, 1940-
    The all-new clean joke book / Bob Phillips.
    Summary: A collection of jokes arranged alphabet-
ically by topic.
    ISBN 0-89081-830-4
    1. American wit and humor.   [1. Jokes.]
    I. Title.
    PN6162.P455   1990   90-36617
    818'.5402—dc20   CIP
                                         AC

Printed in the United States of America.

Other Books by Bob Phillips

ABOVE AVERAGE

Wife: Scientists claim that the average person speaks 10,000 words a day.

Husband: Yes, dear, but remember, you are far above the average.

ABSENT-MINDED

The absent-minded professor of biology said to his class: "I have in this sack, an excellent specimen of a frog that I dissected."

When he opened the sack he pulled out a sandwich and a cupcake. "Strange," he said, "I think I have already eaten lunch."

ACCIDENT

An insurance agent was writing a policy for a zookeeper. "Have you ever had any accidents?"

"No," said the zookeeper. "But once a rattlesnake bit me and an elephant stepped on my foot."

"Don't you call those accidents?" asked the insurance agent.

"No," replied the zookeeper, "they did it on purpose."

ACTING

"Stop acting like a fool!"

"I'm not acting!"

ACTOR

Did you hear about the actor that fell off a ship as it was passing near a lighthouse? The poor fellow drowned because he persisted in swimming in circles in order to keep within the spotlight.

ADVERTISING

It pays to advertise. Did you know that there are 25 mountains in Colorado higher than Pike's Peak which few people could name?

*   *   *

Winking at a girl in the dark is like doing business without advertising. You know what you are doing, but nobody else does.

*   *   *

Bill: Do you think your advertising has done any good?

Pete: Yes indeed. Why only the other day I advertised for a night watchman and that very night my store was robbed.

ALLOWANCE

Boy: I want to marry your daughter.

Dad: How much money do you make?

Bob: Two hundred dollars a month.

Dad: Well, her allowance is 150 dollars a month—and that'll make...

Bob: No, I've already figured that in.

AMATEURS

I have always been confused when I hear the phrase "professional women"—are there any amateurs?

ANGEL

Melba: The King of England struck one of my ancestors on the shoulder with the tip of his sword and made him a knight.

Pam: That's nothing! My grandfather was walking next to a new building when one of the carpenters dropped his hammer. It struck my grandfather on the head and made him an angel.

* * *

Did you hear about the dead angel? He died of harp failure.

ANTIQUES

Being an antique dealer is a strange way to make a living. It's the only business where grandparents buy something, the parents sell it, and the grandchildren buy it again.

ANTS

Teacher: Why were you so late for school?
Student: I had to say good-bye to my pets.
Teacher: But you were two hours late.
Student: I have a large ant farm.

* * *

Teacher: Children, we can learn from the ants. Ants work very hard every day. The ant works all the time. And what happens in the end?
Student: Somebody steps on him.

APOLOGIZE

Father: I see you got a D for conduct but an A for courtesy. How is that possible?
Son: Whenever I kick someone I apologize.

APRIL FOOL

Joe: When were you born?
Moe: April 2nd.
Joe: I see. One day too late!

APPLAUSE

Friend: You received a tremendous ovation. In fact, they are still clapping. What did you say?

Speaker: I told them I would not go on with my speech until they quieted down.

* * *

George: When I left the stage, the audience went wild with applause.

Harry: That's because they knew you weren't coming back!

ARTIST

Model: The light's too strong. This chair is too hard. I can't stand this dress. My hair's a mess. My lipstick is the wrong color.

Artist: What is your name?

Model: Lisa.

So the painter called the work "The Moaner Lisa."

AUSTRALIA

An American was knocked unconscious in a traffic accident in Australia. The ambulance took him to a local hospital. When he finally woke up he asked the nurse, "Was I brought here to die?"

"No," said the nurse, "you were brought in here yesterdye."

BACKSLIDING

A tramp knocked at a farmer's door and asked for some food.

"Are you a Christian?" asked the farmer.

"Of course," said the tramp. "Can't you tell? Just look at the knees of my pants. Don't they prove it?"

The farmer and his wife noticed the holes in the knees and promptly gave the man some food.

As the tramp turned to go the farmer asked, "By the way, what made those holes in the seat of your pants?"

"Backsliding," said the tramp.

BAD LUCK

Marty: Do you believe that you will get seven years of bad luck if you break a mirror?

Larry: Of course not. My uncle broke a mirror and he didn't have seven years of bad luck.

Marty: He didn't?

Larry: No, he was hit by a car that same day.

BAIL

Judge: What terrible crime has this man committed?

Lawyer: He has not done anything wrong. He was merely an innocent bystander when the killer shot a clerk in a hold-up. We are holding him as a witness.

Judge: And where is the killer?
Lawyer: He's out on bail.

BALD

Ken: I find that split hair is a problem.
Bob: Yeah, you're right. Mine split about five years ago.

BANANAS

Joe: What did the banana say to the elephant?
Moe: I don't know.
Joe: Nothing. Bananas can't talk.

BANKRUPT

Did you hear about the dating agency for chickens? It went bankrupt. They couldn't make hens meet.

BARBER

Customer: Before you begin, I want you to know that I like the weather that we are having, I have no interest in baseball or football, I do not want to hear who won the prize fights, I am not interested in the latest newspaper scandals, and I don't want to discuss political issues. Now, go ahead with your work.

Barber: Okay. And if it won't offend you, sir, I will be able to do my work better and faster if you don't talk so much.

*　　*　　*

Barber: Haven't I shaved you before, sir?
Customer: No, I got this scar in the war.

BASEBALL

Although (insert name of baseball player) was not a good fielder, he was not a good hitter, either.

*   *   *

One young woman at her first baseball game said that she liked the pitcher the best "because he hit the bat every time."

BATHING

Mark: How about a song?
Ryan: Who me?
Mark: Yeah.
Ryan: Not me. I only do my singing in the shower.
Mark: Don't sing very often, do you?

BEARD

Paul: I once had a beard like yours, and when I saw how terrible I looked, I immediately cut it off.
Saul: I used to have a face like yours, too. And when I saw how terrible it made me look, I immediately grew a beard.

BED

Landlady: I charge $30.00 a night, and only $15.00 if you make your own bed.

Guest: I'll make my own bed.

Landlady: Hang on. I'll get you a hammer and nails.

BIG-GAME HUNTER

Little John: I used to be a big-game hunter. Why, for years I shot elephants in Alaska.

Big Alfred: That's impossible! There aren't any elephants in Alaska.

Little John: Of course not. I shot them all.

BIG HOLES

Harry: What do you get when you cross an elephant and a mouse?

Cary: I don't know.

Harry: I don't know either, but it sure makes big holes in the walls.

BILL

Virginia: When was your son born?

Beverly: In March. He came on the first of the month.

Virginia: Is that why you call him Bill?

BILLIARD TABLE

Rob: What is four yards long, has six legs, and would kill you if it fell out of a tree?
Ted: I don't know.
Rob: A billiard table.

BLAME

It is very warm and reassuring to know that when you get married, no matter what comes along, you'll always have somebody at your side to blame it on.

BLIND

Love is said to be blind, but I know lots of fellows who can see twice as much in their sweethearts as I can.

BLONDES

Jean: Do you think she is a natural blonde or a bleached blonde?
Zona: I think she's a suicide blonde.
Jean: What kind is that?
Zona: Dyed by her own hand.

BOAST

Bob was very tired of his friend Ken, who was always name-dropping.

"If you're such a big shot, why don't you go over to the phone, call the White House, and get the President on the line?"

"Okay," said Ken. He punched in a number and in a few seconds someone answered the phone. Ken handed the phone to Bob.

"Hello, this is the president," said the familiar voice on the other end.

Bob thought it was a trick.

"Okay, that was impressive," said Bob. "But if you are really such a hotshot, why don't you call Buckingham Palace and let me talk with the queen?"

Ken went back to the phone and punched in a number and handed the receiver to Bob.

"Hello," came a distinctive voice. "This is the Queen of England speaking."

Bob was very impressed, but still very suspicious.

"All right, you happen to know the president and the queen. But if you're really a big deal, you'll get the pope on the phone."

"I'll do better than that," said Ken. Ken took Bob to the airport and they boarded a plane to the Vatican. There Ken disappeared, leaving Bob to mill about with the crowd in St. Peter's Square.

Suddenly the crowd became silent. Bob followed everyone's gaze to a balcony, where Ken and the pope stood side by side.

Before Bob could recover from his amazement, a man standing beside him poked him in the ribs.

With a heavily accented voice the man asked "Who's that up there on the balcony with Ken?"

BOOING

Two speakers were on the same program. One of them did an outstanding job of delivery. The other speaker was boring. The boring speaker was overheard saying, "Poor Dr. Wilson, he's having it pretty rough. He spoke before I did and he didn't go over at all. In fact, the crowd didn't like him—they booed and hissed the poor fellow right off the stage. He was so bad that right in the middle of my speech, they started booing him again!"

BORE

Young man: Yes, I know a great deal about baseball and football. I was also the captain of our basketball team. I drive race cars and motorcycles. I can swim and dance and I'm sure that you would have a great time going out on a date with me. I am a good conversationalist.

Young lady: Do you have a group photograph of yourself?

*　　*　　*

Bore: I shot this lion in Africa. It was a case of him or me.

Bored: Well, the lion certainly makes a better rug.

BOXING

Boxing coach: You did a terrible job out there. If I were as big as you, I would be heavyweight champion of the world.

Boxer: Why don't you become the lightweight champion?

BRAGGING

Friend: Has your son's education proved valuable?

Father: Yes, it has. It has cured his mother of bragging about him.

BRAINS

Dave: My girlfriend's really smart. She has brains enough for two.

Jeff: Sounds like the right girl for you.

BRICK

Patient: My feet are always cold.

Doctor: Well, all you have to do is go to bed and have a brick at your feet.

Patient: I tried that.

Doctor: Did you get the brick hot?

Patient: Get it hot? It took me all night just to get it warm.

BROKER

Get my broker, Miss Smith.

Yes, sir—stock or pawn?

BUMS

Two bums were discussing the reasons they became bums.

"I'm the fellow who never listened to anybody," said the first bum.

"Shake, partner," said the second bum. "I'm the man who followed everybody's advice."

BURGLAR ALARM

George: My dad's very rich, so I don't know what to give him for Christmas. What do you give to a man who has everything?

Harold: A burglar alarm.

BUSINESS

Art: How's business?

Ted: Terrible. Even the people who never pay have stopped buying.

BUTCHER

Customer: Look, you are giving me a big piece of bone. With meat as expensive as i is, I don't want all that bone.

Butcher: I'm not giving it to you, lady, you're paying for it.

* * *

Woman: I want a piece of beef, and make it lean.

Butcher: Certainly, madam. Which way?

CAGED UP

A family of lions feeding in the African Safari Park

looked up as a car crammed with eight tourists pulled close to them.

"It's cruel," said the papa lion to his family, "to keep them caged up like that!"

CALENDAR

Jess: Did you hear about the fellow who stole the calendar?

Ray: No, what happened?

Jess: He got 12 months.

CAMP LETTERS

Dear Mom and Dad,

Camp is okay, I think. We went hiking yesterday. Send my other tennis shoe if you can.

Love,
Robbie

*　　*　　*

Dear Mom and Dad,

The camp Director is making everyone write home.

Tammy

*　　*　　*

Dear Mom and Dad,

When you made me go to camp, I told you something bad and terrible would happen to me. And I was right. It did happen.

Love,
George

*   *   *

CAMP ITCHAGOOY
Hideaway Village, Washington

Dear Mr. and Mrs. Phillips:

Your daughter Lisa is having a terrific time at camp. Everyone on the staff thinks she is great. She is very popular with everyone in her cabin. We just wanted you to know how much we appreciate having her at Camp Itchagooy. You can be very proud of her.

Most Sincerely,
David Ferriera
Director

R. E. Phillips
2972 East Willson Ave.,
Willacke, Washington

Dear Mr. Ferriera:

My wife and I were very excited and pleased to learn that Lisa was having a fun time at camp. Being popular is very important. We are most proud of Lisa.

We have a daughter at Camp Itchagooy, too. Her name

is Christy. It would be very nice of you to let us know how she is doing.

Warmly yours,
R.E. Phillips, Father

CANNIBAL

Most cannibal jokes aren't in good taste.

CANOE

Teacher: If I write n-e-w on the blackboard, what does it spell?
Student: New.
Teacher: Now, I'll put a "k" in front of it and what do we have?
Student: Canoe.

CAPITALISM

Russian economist: I went over to the United States to study the death of capitalism.
Russian leader: What are your conclusions?
Russian economist: What a wonderful way to die.

CAPTAIN

A young man made a great deal of money in real estate. He decided to buy himself a small yacht. He then bought the proper clothes and decked himself out in the regalia of a captain.

His first visitor on board his new yacht was his grandmother. He took her on a tour of the boat. In the process, the grandson pointed to his cap with crossed anchors on it and said, "This signifies that I am a captain."

The grandmother made no comment.

"You don't seem very impressed," said the young man.

"If you want me to be impressed, I'll be impressed," said his grandmother. "To yourself, you're a captain. To me, you're maybe a captain. But to captains, you're no captain."

CASH

As for money, it's only called cold cash because it doesn't stay in your pocket long enough to get warm.

CATS

Heckle: Did you ever see the Catskill mountains?

Jeckle: No, but I've seen what cats do to mice.

CEMETERY

Gary: Why are cemeteries in the middle of some towns?

Larry: Because they are dead centers.

CHANCES

You have two chances: one of getting the germ, and one of not getting the germ. If you get the germ, you have two chances: one of getting the disease, and one of not getting the disease. If you get the disease, you have two chances: one of dying, and one of not dying. And if you die—well, you still have two chances.

CHANGE

Scott: I went to a hotel for a change and rest.
Tim: Did you get it?
Scott: The bellboy got the change and the hotel got the rest.

*   *   *

Fred: When I was twenty I made up my mind to get rich.
Carl: But you never became rich.
Fred: No. I decided it was easier to change my mind.

CHARACTER

"How do you like the new minister?" a customer asked one of the town merchants.

"I haven't heard him preach, but I like him fine," said the merchant.

"How can you like him if you haven't heard him?"

"I know that he is good, because everyone is beginning to pay off their bills!"

CHESS

"Did you hear that the Russian chess champion died after he lost the game to an American?"

"When did that happen?"
"Tomorrow."

CHILD ABUSE

A little boy was about to be spanked by his father.
"Did Grandpa spank you when you were little?"
"Yes, he did."
"Did Grandpa's father spank him?"
"Yes."
"And did Great-grandpa's father spank him?"
"He probably did."
"Well," said the boy, "Don't you think it's about time to stop this inherited child abuse?"

CIGARS

A defendant in a lawsuit involving a large sum of money was talking to his lawyer.

"If I loose the case, I'll be ruined," he said.

"It's in the judge's hands now." said the lawyer.

"Would it help if I sent the judge a box of cigars?"

"Oh, no," said the lawyer. "This judge is a stickler for ethical behavior. A stunt like that would prejudice him against you. He might even hold you in contempt of court. In fact, you shouldn't even smile at the judge."

Within the course of time, the judge rendered a decision in favor of the defendant.

As the defendant left the courthouse with his lawyer he said, "Thanks for the tip about the cigars. It worked."

"I'm sure we would have lost the case if you had sent them."

"But I did send them."

"You did?"

"Yes. That is how we won the case."

"I don't understand," said the lawyer.

"It's easy. I sent the cigars to the judge, but enclosed my opponent's business card."

CIVIL SERVANT

Q. What is the difference between a chess player and a civil servant?

A. A chess player moves every now and then.

COACH

During the review of the football plays before a big game, one of the star running backs spent most of the time reading a comic book. The coach noticed but didn't say anything about it.

It was a very exciting and important game, but the coach made the running back sit on the bench until the last quarter. When the last quarter started the coach said to the running back, "Warm up!"

After a series of warm-up moves, the running back said, "I'm ready, coach."

The coach reached into his coat pocket and pulled out a comic book. "Here," he said. "Sit over there at the end of the bench and read it."

COCKROACH

Customer: Do you have any cockroaches?

Sporting goods store owner: Yes, we sell them to fishermen.

Customer: I would like 20,000 of them.

Sporting goods store owner: What do you want with 20,000 cockroaches?

Customer: I'm moving tomorrow and my lease says I must leave my apartment in the same condition in which I found it.

COCONUT

New bride: I fixed your favorite dessert for you tonight—coconut pudding. Wait until you see it."

New groom: Wow! That's great! But what's that big lump in the middle?

New bride: That's the coconut.

COINCIDENCE

Harry: What does coincidence mean?

Larry: Funny, I was just going to ask you that same question.

COLD

Q. Which travels faster—heat or cold?

A. Heat....Because you can catch cold.

COLD CUTS

"You're only as old as you think."
"In that case you must be about three months old."

* * *

You have a striking personality. How long has it been on strike?

* * *

You're not really such a bad person—until people get to know you.

* * *

Of course I'm listening to you; don't you see me yawning?

* * *

I've enjoyed talking to you; my mind needed the rest.

* * *

Is that your head, or did somebody find a way to grow hair on a meatball?

* * *

Ordinarily he was insane, but he had lucid moments when he was merely stupid.

* * *

I'd like to give you something you need, but I don't know how to wrap up a bathtub.

*   *   *

You talk so much I get hoarse just listening to you.

*   *   *

While he was not dumber than an ox, he was not any smarter either.

*   *   *

You really have a head on your shoulders. Too bad it's on backward.

*   *   *

You're such a bore, even my leg falls asleep when you talk.

*   *   *

Did I miss you when you were gone? I didn't know you were gone.

*   *   *

The only time you make sense is when you're not talking.

*   *   *

You may not be light on your feet, but you certainly are light in your head.

*   *   *

I think you're the greatest, but then again, what do I know?

*   *   *

"Some boys think I'm pretty and some think I'm ugly. What do you think?"
"A bit of both."

*   *   *

"They say two heads are better than one."
"In your case, none is better than one."

*   *   *

Things could be worse—you could be here in person.

*   *   *

You're a person of few words—a few million words.

*   *   *

There are two reasons why you don't mind your own business: 1) no mind; and 2) no business.

*   *   *

Travel broadens a person. You look like you've been all over the world.

* * *

I didn't say he was dumb—I said he was 16 years old before he could wave good-bye.

* * *

"Do you think I'm a fool?"
"No, but what's my opinion against thousands of others?"

* * *

"Excuse me—I was lost in thought."
"Yes, it's always easy to get lost where one is a stranger."

* * *

"Do you believe it is possible to communicate with the dead?"
"Yes, I can hear you distinctly."

* * *

"I live by my wits."
"Now I know why you look so hungry."

* * *

"If you refuse me, I'll blow my brains out."
"Oh, how could you?"

*   *   *

"What would the world be without its little joke?"
"You wouldn't be alive."

COMEBACK

Two editors of local newspapers did not get along
and used their newspapers to do battle.

"The editor of the *Daily Express* is mean enough to
steal the swill from a blind hog," wrote the editor of
the *Daily Post*.

The next day the following appeared in the *Daily
Express.*

"The editor of the *Daily Post* knows that we never
stole his swill."

COMMUTERS

Two elderly women on a commuter train got into an
argument about the window: One insisted that it had
to be open or she would suffocate; the other demanded
that it be closed so she would not catch a cold. The
conductor was asked to settle the noisy dispute.

A commuter nearby called to the conductor, "Open
the window first, and let one of them catch cold and
die. Then close it and let the other one suffocate."

COMPLAIN

Wife one: Does your husband kick about his meals?

Wife two: No. What he kicks about is having to get them.

COMPUTER

Joe: I was selected by a computer as an ideal boyfriend.

Moe: Who wants to be a computer's boyfriend?

CONCEITED

"So your sister got fired?"

"Yes. But she was going to leave anyway. Her boss is so conceited—he thinks the words can only be spelled his way."

CONGRESS

"Reader, suppose you were an idiot. And suppose you were a member of Congress. But I repeat myself."
—Mark Twain

CONTACTS

Salesman one: I made some very valuable contacts today.

Salesman two: I didn't make any sales, either.

CONTEMPT

A famous trial lawyer was asked to apologize to the court for some remarks he had made. With dignity, he bowed to the judge and said: "Your Honor is right, and I am wrong, as Your Honor generally is."

The judge never figured out whether he should be satisfied with this remark or cite the lawyer for contempt of court.

*   *   *

A lawyer was questioning the testimony of a witness to a shooting.

"Did you see the shot fired?"

"No, sir, I only heard it."

"Stand down," said the judge sharply. "Your testimony is of no value."

The witness turned around in the box to leave, and when his back was turned to the judge he laughed loud and derisively. Irate at this exhibition of contempt, the judge called the witness back to the chair and demanded to know how he dared to laugh at the court.

"Did you see me laugh, Judge?" asked the witness.

"No, but I heard you," retorted the judge.

"That evidence is not satisfactory, Your Honor," said the witness respectfully.

CONTEMPTIBLE

Student: Professor, my opinion of you is most contemptible.

Professor: Sir, I never knew an opinion of yours that was not contemptible.

CONTRIBUTION

An artist was asked to contribute to a church fund drive. "I'm sorry, but I'm broke," he explained, "but I'll contribute a $400 picture."

The drive was almost complete when the minister came back to the artist. "We are still short $100 for the fund drive. Could you please help?"

"Of course," said the artist. "I'll increase the price of my picture to $500."

COOKING

"Some people can cook but don't."
"My wive can't cook but does."

CORONER

The motorist approached the coroner at 75-miles-per-hour.

COUNTESS

A newspaper columnist was found guilty and fined for calling a countess a cow. When the trial ended and the man paid his fine, he asked the judge if, since it was now clear he could not call a countess a cow, he could call a cow a countess.

The judge said that that was all right to do. Whereupon the newspaperman turned toward the countess in the courtroom, bowed elaborately, and said, "How do you do, Countess."

COUNTDOWN

Overheard at the rocket launchpad control room: "He's a fine fellow practically all of the time, but he is inclined to blow-up without any countdown."

CRAZY

Patient: Doctor, people are always calling me crazy. It makes me very angry.

Psychiatrist: Perhaps you ought to start at the beginning....

Patient: Okay. In the beginning, I created the heavens and the earth. And the earth was without form and void....

*   *   *

Psychiatrist: I'm afraid you are crazy.

Patient: Well, are you all right?

Psychiatrist: Certainly, I'm all right.

Patient: Then I'm glad I'm crazy.

CREDIT

The man of the 20th century is one who drives a mortgaged car over a bond-financed highway on credit-card gas.

CREDITORS

"Would you be happy if you had all the money you wanted?"

"I'd be happy if I had all the money my creditors wanted."

CRICKETS

Bob: The national sport in Spain is bullfighting and in England it's cricket.

Ray: I'd rather play in England.

Bob: Why do you say that?

Ray: It's easier to fight crickets.

CUTIE PIE

One afternoon the boss' wife met him at the office. As they were going down the elevator it stopped, and a luscious blonde secretary got on, poked the boss in the ribs, and said, "Hello, cutie pie."

The wife, without blinking, leaned over and said, "I'm Mrs. Pie."

DAFFY DEFINITIONS

ADMIRATION: Our polite recognition of another person's resemblance to ourselves.

ADOLESCENCE: The period in which the young suddenly feel a great responsibility about answering the telephone.

ADOLESCENCE: The period when children are certain they will never be as dumb as their parents.

ADOLESCENT: A teenager who acts like a baby when you don't treat him like an adult.

AMERICANS: People with more timesaving devices and less time than any other people in the world.

ANTIDOTE: The medicine that kills dotes.

BABY: An angel whose wings decrease as his legs increase.

BABY: An alimentary canal with a loud voice at one end and no responsibility at the other.

BACHELOR: A rolling stone that gathers no boss.

BACHELOR GIRL: A girl who is still looking for a bachelor.

BANKER: A fellow who lends you his umbrella when the sun is shining and wants it back the minute it begins to rain.

BANKER: A pawnbroker with a manicure.

BORE: Someone who, upon leaving a room, makes you feel that someone fascinating just walked in.

BUDGET: A method of worrying before you spend as well as afterward.

BUDGET: A schedule for going into debt systematically.

BUDGET: An attempt to live below your yearnings.

BUS FARE: Jack-in-the-box.

CLOVERLEAF: California's state flower.

CLARITY: The ability to give directions without taking your hands out of your pockets.

COACH: A fellow who is always willing to lay down your life for his job.

CRITIC: A legless man who teaches running.

DENTIST: A magician who puts metal into your mouth, and pulls coins out of your pocket.

DERMATOLOGIST: A person who makes rash judgments.

DIET: The penalty for exceeding the feed limit.

DIPLOMACY: The art of saying "nice doggie" until you have time to pick up a rock.

DISARMAMENT: An agreement between nations to scuttle all weapons that are obsolete.

ECONOMIST: A man who knows more about money than people who have it.

EDITOR: A person employed on a newspaper, whose business is to separate the wheat from the chaff—and see that the chaff is printed.

EFFICIENCY EXPERT: The person who is smart enough to tell you how to run your business and too smart to start one of his own.

ELOCUTION: A form of punishment whereby many people are put to death.

ETERNAL TRIANGLE: Diapers.

EXPERIENCE: The name we give our mistakes.

FLATTERY: A collection of flats.

FRIENDSHIP: An emotion so sweet, steady, loyal, and enduring that it lasts an entire lifetime—unless asked to lend money.

FURTHERMORE: It is much farther than "further."

HONEYMOON: The vacation a man takes before beginning work under a new boss.

HOSPITAL BED: A parked taxi with the meter running.

HUNCH: What you call an idea that you're afraid is wrong.

IGNORAMUS: Someone who doesn't know something that you learned yesterday.

INCENTIVE: The possibility of getting more money than you earn.

INSOMNIA: What a person has when he lies awake all night for an hour.

INSURANCE: Paying for catastrophes on the installment plan.

ITALICS: The language spoken by ancient Italians.

LAME DUCK: A politician whose goose has been cooked.

LIFE INSURANCE: A contract that keeps you poor so you can die rich.

MARKET ANALYST: A person who tells you what is going to happen within six months and then after that tells you why it didn't.

METALLURGIST: Someone who is allergic to iron.

MILLIONAIRE: A man who leaves his air-conditioned home, enters his air-conditioned car to be driven to his air-conditioned office, where he works until he leaves to have lunch in an air-conditioned restaurant, and then at the end of the day rides in his air-conditioned car to his air-conditioned club, where he goes into the steam room for an hour to sweat.

MURDERER: One who is presumed innocent until he is proved insane.

NURSERY: A school for nurses.

OPTIMIST: A man who goes into a restaurant without a dime and figures on paying for the meal with the pearl he hopes to find in the oyster.

ORATORY: The art of making deep noises from the chest sound like important messages from the brain.

PACIFIST: A guy who fights with everybody but the enemy.

PEDIATRICIANS: Men of little patients.

PANTRY: A collection of pants.

PAST TENSE: When you used to be nervous.

PAWNBROKER: One who lives off the flat of the land.

PLANNING: The art of putting off until tomorrow what you have no intention of doing today.

PROFESSOR: One who talks in someone else's sleep.

PSYCHOLOGIST: A man who, when a good-looking girl enters the room, looks at everybody else.

QUININE: A valuable medicine that comes from barking trees.

RELATIVITY: When you are with a pretty girl for three hours, and it seems like only three minutes, and then you sit on a hot stove for a minute and think it's an hour.

RICH MAN: One who isn't afraid to ask the clerk to show him something cheaper.

REPARTEE: Something great we think of 24 hours too late.

RESORTS: Places where people go for change and rest. And where the waiters get all the change and the landlord gets the rest.

SARCASM: Barbed ire.

SINKING FUND: A place where they hide the profits from the stockholders.

SPECIALIST: A doctor whose patients are expected to confine their ailments to his office hours.

STATISTICIAN: A liar who can figure.

STOCKBROKER: A man who can take a bankroll and run it into a shoestring.

TACT: Thinking all you say without saying all you think.

TACT: The art of saying nothing when there is nothing to say.

TAXPAYER: One who doesn't have to pass a civil service exam to work for the government.

UPPER CRUST: A lot of crumbs held together by dough.

UNIVERSITY: An institution for the postponement of experience.

VIRUS: A Latin medical term meaning, "Your guess is as good as mine."

WAITER: A man who thinks money grows on trays.

YAWN: A silent shout.

ZOO: A place devised for animals to study the habits of human beings.

DAMP

Joe: Why was your letter so damp?
Moe: Postage due, I guess.

DAREDEVIL

Two local dairies engaged in an advertising war. One hired a daredevil driver to drive a car around town with a large sign reading:

THIS DAREDEVIL DRINKS OUR MILK.

The rival company came out with a larger sign reading:

YOU DON'T HAVE TO BE A DAREDEVIL
TO DRINK OUR MILK.

DARN

First husband: Well, I can tell you're a married man all right. No holes in your stockings now.

Second husband: No. One of the first things my wife taught me was how to darn them.

DEAD

Mr. Hanson died on the golf course, and no one wanted to tell his wife the bad news. Finally a friend placed the call.

"Joan," he said, "Richard lost $5000 playing poker."

"What!" she screamed. "He should drop dead."

"Funny you should mention that...."

DEADBEAT

A doctor spotted a deadbeat patient while he was out to dinner. He called the patient aside and reminded him that he owed $250 for the work done more than two years earlier. He insisted that the man pay up. To the doctor's astonishment, the patient pulled a check-book from his pocket and wrote a check to the doctor for the full amount.

Skeptical about the man's good faith, the doctor went directly to the bank the next morning and presented the check for payment. The teller handed back the check with the explanation that the patient's account was $25 short of the amount of the check. The dentist smiled, stepped back to the customer's desk for a few minutes, came back to the teller, deposited $35 to the account of his former patient, and then again presented the $250 check. He walked out with a net gain of $215.

DEAD LETTER

Howard: What's that peculiar odor I smell around this post office?

George: Probably the dead letters.

DEMOCRATS

The rumor was started that the democrats were against religion and for atheism. In fact, they might even destroy the Bible.

An old lady, wondering how the Scriptures could be preserved in such an event, called on a democrat friend in her town and asked him to hide her Bible.

After scoffing at the idea that democrats would suppress and destroy all the Bibles, the democrat asked the old lady why she wanted him to hide her Bible.

"Because, she said, "they'll never think of looking for a Bible in the house of a democrat."

*   *   *

I never said all democrats were saloonkeepers; what I said was all saloonkeepers were democrats.

DENTIST

Dentist: Do you want the good news or the bad news?

Patient: Give me the good news.

Dentist: Your teeth are perfect.

Patient: What's the bad news?

Dentist: Your gums are so bad that I'll have to take all your teeth out.

*   *   *

Patient: Hey, that wasn't the tooth I wanted pulled.

Dentist: Calm yourself, I'm coming to it!

*   *   *

Mrs Williams wasn't very happy about having her tooth pulled, but the dentist assured her there was no other choice. Nonetheless, every time he went to put the forceps in her mouth, she clenched her teeth.

Whispering to the nurse, the dentist tried again. At the instant he approached her, the nurse pinched Mrs. Williams on the bottom with all her strength. The woman's mouth opened wide, and the tooth was pulled.

"Now," the dentist said when it was all over, "that wasn't so bad."

"No," Mrs. Williams agreed. "But who would have imagined that the roots went so far down!"

DEPRESSED

Scott: What makes this milk so blue?

Mike: Because it comes from discontented cows.

DIAMOND RING

Mr. Smith bought a beautiful diamond ring for his wife and at lunch showed it to his friend Mr. Jones.

Jones offered to buy it for more than Smith had paid. Smith later regretted the sale and bought it back from Jones at a still higher price, but Jones again bought it back from Smith at a much higher price. Finally Jones sold the ring to a person unknown to Smith.

When Smith heard of this final transaction he protested. "How could you do such a stupid thing!" he said. "That was crazy. We were both making such a good living from that ring!"

DICTATION

New boss: Can you take dictation?
Secretary: No, I've never been married.

DIET

Did you hear about the sword swallower who went on a diet? He was on pins and needles for six months.

DIFFERENCE

Teacher: What's the difference between a porpoise and a dolphin?
Student: That's what I say, What's the difference?

DINING ROOM

Rob: Why do you have your front door leading right into your dining room?
Jim: So my wife's relatives won't have to waste any time.

DIPHTHERIA

Mary: Are you ever troubled with diphtheria?
Sally: Only when I try to spell it.

DISCRETION

Man: Pardon me, young lady, but in the matter of dress, don't you think you could show a little more discretion?
Girl: My gosh, some of you guys are never satisfied.

*　　*　　*

Q. What is the difference between valor and discretion?
A. To travel on an ocean liner without tipping would be valor. To come back on a different ocean liner would be discretion.

DOCTOR, DOCTOR

Gary: Only last week they took my poor brother off to the hospital.
Larry: What are they going to do for him?
Gary: They're going to operate.
Larry: What for?
Gary: Twelve hundred dollars.
Larry: What did he have?

Gary: Twelve hundred dollars
Larry: What was the complaint?
Gary: No complaint. Everybody was satisfied.

*   *   *

The nurse burst into the doctor's office. "Dr. Poure!" she yelled. "You just gave Mr. Weston a clean bill of health . . . and he dropped dead right outside the door on his way out."

Dr. Poure leaped into action. "Quick," he said. "We've got to turn him around so it looks like he was just coming in."

*   *   *

My wife was very sick so we called Doctor Griffin. He gave her some medicine and she got worse. I then called Doctor Kurth and he gave her some more medicine and she still got worse. I thought she was going to die, so I called Doctor Cross and he was too busy, and finally my wife got well.

*   *   *

Doctor: There goes the only woman I ever loved.
Nurse: Why don't you marry her?
Doctor: I can't afford to. She's my best patient.

*   *   *

First boy: A little bird told me what kind of lawyer your father is.
Second boy: What did he say?

First boy: Cheep! Cheep!
Second boy: Oh, yeah. Well, a duck just told me what kind of doctor your father is.

*　　*　　*

Doctor: Just do as I say, and you'll be another man.
Patient: Okay, and Doctor, don't forget to send your bill to the other man.

*　　*　　*

Patient one: How many doctors does it take to screw in a light bulb?
Patient two: How many?
Patient one: It depends on whether or not the bulb has health insurance.

*　　*　　*

My doctor is a very generous man. He gave me four months to live. When I told him that I didn't think I would be able to pay his bill before I died, he gave me another six months.

*　　*　　*

Patient: Doctor, how long can a person live without a brain?
Doctor: I give up. How old are you?

*　　*　　*

Patient: Doc, am I getting better?
Doctor: I don't know—let me feel your purse.

*　　*　　*

Husband: Darling, I went in and paid the doctor another $50 today.

Wife: Isn't that wonderful! Just think, three more payments and the baby will be ours.

*   *   *

Patient: Doctor, how can I broaden my mind?

Doctor: How about a stick of dynamite between your ears?

*   *   *

Patient: Doc, what's the difference between an itch and an allergy?

Doctor: About 35 dollars.

*   *   *

Then there is the story about the man who wanted a corn removed. The corn was painful so he went to the hospital. Since he thought the removal might be painful, he asked for an anesthetic. Once the anesthetic was applied, his heart stopped. The frantic doctors immediately operated and conducted a heart massage to revive the man.

Though the regular heartbeat was soon restored, the patient had been given such an overdose of oxygen that additional surgery was required to relieve a stomach swelling. Two operations later, the patient was being returned to the recovery room when the elevator jammed. The interns had to place him on a stretcher. During this maneuver, an intern slipped and the man crashed to the floor, breaking his arm and collarbone. The man suddenly began gasping for air. He was rushed to the operation room for his third operation of the day, a tracheotomy.

During all the confusion, the doctors forgot to remove his corn.

*　　*　　*

Woman: I wish you would see my husband. He's out of his mind. He blows smoke rings all the time.
Doctor: That's not unusual, I do that myself.
Woman: But Doctor, he doesn't smoke.

*　　*　　*

Patient: Doctor, I think I'm a bridge.
Doctor: What on earth's come over you?
Patient: So far, ten cars, three buses and a truck.

*　　*　　*

Patient: Doctor, I keep seeing frogs in front of my eyes.
Doctor: Don't worry. It's only a hoptical illusion.

*　　*　　*

Patient: I think I'm a slice of bread.
Doctor: You'll have to stop loafing around.

*　　*　　*

Patient: Doctor, I think that there are two of me.

Doctor: Why don't you both sit down and one of you tell me about it.

*   *   *

Patient: I have this desperate urge to paint myself gold.

Doctor: I think it must be a gilt complex.

*   *   *

Doctor: If I find it necessary to operate, would you have the money to pay for it?

Patient: If I didn't have the money, would you find it necessary to operate?

*   *   *

A man mistook an insane asylum for a college. When his error was pointed out to him he said to the attendant, "Well, I don't suppose there's much difference."

"There's a big difference, Mister," said the attendant. "Here you have to show improvement before you get out."

*   *   *

One day a well-to-do society lady visited a mental hospital. As she was walking around, a distinguished-looking man offered his services as a guide on her tour.

In the course of several hours of careful inspection the society lady became impressed by the knowledge and intelligence of her guide. She was pleased by his gentle manners and obvious good breeding. In taking her leave she thanked him and expressed her belief that the hospital was in good hands.

"Oh, but I am not a hospital official," the man said. "I am a patient." He then told her how he had been unjustly committed by greedy members of his family who only had designs on his personal fortune. His detailed and reasonable account of the conspiracy touched the society woman's heart. She thought that it was a terrible wrong for the man to have been committed. She promised to get help and go to a judge to correct whatever injustice had been done. The kindly man thanked her for her warm kindness.

As she turned to go down the steps, she received a vigorous kick in the bottom. This caused her to stumble and nearly fall down the entire flight of stairs.

Gasping and in shock, she turned toward the man and demanded, "Why did you do that? I might have been seriously hurt."

The patient smiled gently. "I didn't want to hurt you. I did that so you would not forget to tell the judge about my case."

*   *   *

A man went to a psychiatrist to seek some help for depression. As he entered the reception room he noticed two doors marked "Men" and "Women." He went through the door marked "Men."

He then encountered two other doors marked "Extrovert" and "Introvert." He decided that he was an introvert and opened that door. He found himself in a room with two more doors marked "Those Making $40,000 and Over" and "Those Making Less than $40,000."

He knew that he made less than $40,000, so he opened that door. He found himself outside the building.

*   *   *

Patient: Every night when I get into bed I think that someone is under my bed. I then get up and look. There is never anyone there. When I crawl under the bed and lie down, I get the idea that there is someone on top of the bed. I then get up and look and I never find anyone on top of the bed. This goes on all night, up and down, up and down, it's driving me out of my mind. Do you think you can help?

Psychiatrist: I think I can. All you have to do is visit me twice a week for the next two years and I think I can cure you. The visits will cost $75 an hour.

Patient: That is an awful lot of money for a working man like me. I'll have to talk it over with my wife and let you know.

The next week the patient phoned the psychiatrist.

Patient: I won't be back Doc. My wife solved the problem. She cut the legs off the bed.

*   *   *

Patient: I went to a psychiatrist for six months. I thought I was a dog.

Friend: Well, did you get some help?

Patient: I sure did. I feel great now. Just feel my nose.

*   *   *

A young doctor had just opened his office. His first caller, a stranger, entered. The ambitious doctor asked to be excused as he hurried to the phone. Lifting the receiver he said: "Yes, this is Doctor Vernon. Yes, I'll expect you at ten past two. Please be prompt because I am a very busy man. Yes, the fee will be $600."

Putting down the receiver, he turned to the stranger and said, "Now sir, what can I do for you?"

"Nothing," said the visitor, "I've just come to install the phone."

*　　*　　*

Patient: Doctor, I've got trouble with my throat.

Doctor: Go in the other room and disrobe. I'll be there in a minute.

Patient: But, Doctor, it's just my throat!

Doctor: Get in the other room and disrobe and I'll examine you.

So the man went in and disrobed. As he was sitting there in his shorts, he looked around. Next to him was another guy sitting there in his shorts also, with a big package in his hands.

Patient: Can you imagine that doctor! I've got trouble with my throat and he tells me to disrobe!

Other Man: What are you complaining about? I only came in here to deliver a package!

DO IT NOW

The head of a small industrial concern posted DO IT NOW signs all around his office and plant in the hope of getting better results from his workers. Some weeks later, when asked why he was removing the slogans, he said: "It worked too well: the bookkeeper skipped with $20,000; the chief clerk eloped with the best secretary I've ever had; three salesmen asked for raises; the workers in the factory joined the union and are out on strike; and the office boy threatened to beat me up."

DOUBLE LIFE

First husband: Have you ever suspected your wife of leading a double life?

Second husband: Continually—her own and mine.

DOUBLE THE MONEY

Paperboy: Get your paper right here. Only 50 cents.

Out of town businessman: That' a deal. Why, back home the same paper would cost me twice as much!

Paperboy: You can pay me double if it will help you feel at home.

DOWN

Tom: Do you know how to get down from an elephant?

Jerry: No.

Tom: You don't get down from an elephant; you get down from a duck.

DRAWBACK

First mother: What position does your son play on the football team?

Second mother: I'm not sure. I think he's one of the drawbacks.

DREAM

Writer: I dream up my stories.
Editor: You must dread going to bed.

DRESS

First woman: How do you like my new dress?
Second woman: Fine—but you didn't take the hanger out.
First woman: Those are my shoulder blades.

DRIVING

Policeman: Lady you were doing 85 miles per hour!
Lady: Oh, isn't that splendid. I only learned how to drive yesterday!

DYING

First husband: When I'm near death, I'll ask my wife to cook my last meal.
Second husband: Why?
First Husband: I'll feel more like dying.

ECCENTRICS

Wife: Everyone is talking about the Carlsons' quarrel. Some people are taking his side and others are taking her side.

Husband: And I suppose a few eccentrics are minding their own business.

EGGS

Ralph: Down on our farm, we had a hen lay an egg six inches long.

John: That's nothing. On our farm we can beat that.

Ralph: How?

John: With an egg beater.

* * *

Sales clerk: Those eggs just came from the country.

Shopper: What country?

ELEPHANT

Harry: Why did the elephant paint his toenails different colors?

Cary: I don't know.

Harry: So he could hide in the M&M's.

* * *

Pat: I can lift an elephant with one hand.

Matt: That's impossible.

Pat: No, it's not. Find me an elephant with one hand and I'll prove it.

ETHICS

Son: Dad, what is ethics?

Dad: Well, son, you know that your uncle and I are in business together. Suppose a customer comes in and buys something worth $10 but by mistake gives me a $20 bill and leaves without waiting for his change. If I split the extra $10 with your uncle, that's ethics.

EVOLUTION

Q. How many evolutionists does it take to screw in a light bulb?

A. Just one, but it takes him 200,000 years.

EXERCISE

I get my exercise acting as a pallbearer for my friends who exercise.

* * *

Those who exercise regularly, die healthier.

* * *

Patient: I'm putting on weight, Doctor. What should I do?

Doctor: Regular exercise. Push yourself away from the table three times a day.

EXIT

He gave a tremendous speech. Everyone was moved...toward the exit.

EYE

Policeman: I'm looking for a man with one eye named Carnell.
Bystander: What's his other eye called?

FACE

Nit: Haven't I seen your face somewhere else?
Wit: I don't think so. It has always been between my ears.

* * *

Mother: Your face is clean, but how did you get your hands so dirty?
Son: Washin' my face.

FEET

Teacher: Billy, you've got your shoes on the wrong feet.
Billy: They're the only feet I have.

FICTIONAL

Note from writer to editor: The characters in this novel are entirely fictional and have no resemblance to any person living or dead.

Note from editor to writer: That's what is wrong with them.

FINGERS

My wife bawled me out for eating with my fingers. But I've always said if food wasn't clean enough to pick up with your fingers, it wasn't fit to eat.

*　　*　　*

Sister: Is it good manners to eat chicken with your fingers?

Brother: No, you should eat your fingers separately.

FIT

A distinguished man was invited to a banquet to speak. When he arrived he was placed at the head table. Next to him was an empty chair. The speaker placed his hat on the chair.

A little later, a rather large lady came to the table, pulled out the chair and sat on the speaker's hat. It was crushed as flat as a pancake.

The speaker turned to the woman and said, "Madam, I could have told you that my hat would not fit before you tried it on."

FLAT FEET

Patient: What can I do about my flat feet?
Doctor: Have you tried a foot pump.

FLATHEAD

The teacher told my mother I was a flathead. She was so thrilled that she went all around the neighborhood and bragged about my being so levelheaded.

FOOL

John: Why don't you go to a lawyer with your problem?
Glen: My brother said any fool could advise me, so I came to you.

*   *   *

Wife: I was a fool when I married you.
Husband: I don't doubt it, but I was much too infatuated to notice it.

FOOT

Moe: You're stepping on my foot. Why don't you put your foot where it belongs?
Joe: If I did, you'd go through the door.

FOOTNOTE

Medical Student: There's something written on this patient's foot.
Doctor: That's right. It's a footnote.

FRIENDS

A newly married couple was checking into a hotel-resort. They asked the clerk at the desk to keep their newlywed status a secret.

The next morning the newlyweds were aware of being stared at when they headed for the diner. The groom was very angry and sought out the man at the desk. He rebuked him for passing on the word that they had just been married.

"I never told them that at all," said the clerk. "I just said that you two were good friends."

* * *

Judge: Have you a lawyer?
Prisoner: No, but I have some good friends on the jury.

FROG

Mother: Why did you put this live frog in your sister's bed?
Bob: Because I couldn't find a dead mouse.

FRUIT SALAD

First boy: She had a beautiful pair of eyes, her skin had the glow of a peach, her cheeks were like apples, and her lips like cherries—that's my girl.

Second boy: Sounds like a fruit salad to me.

FURNITURE

Husband: One more payment and the furniture is ours.

Wife: Oh, good. Then we can throw it out and get some new stuff.

GARAGE

Real estate salesman: Could I interest you in a home?

Man: What do I need a home for? I was born in a hospital, educated in a college, courted in an automobile, and married in a church. I live out of tin cans, cellophane bags, and delicatessen stores. I spend my mornings at the office, the afternoons on the golf course, and my evenings at the movies. When I die, I'm going to be buried in the ground. I don't need a home, all I need is a garage.

GAS

"Hello! Is this the City Gas Works?"

"No, this is the Mayor's office."

"Well, I didn't miss it very far, did I?"

GENERATION

Little girl: Mother, you know that vase you said had been handed down from generation to generation?

Mother: Yes.
Little girl: Well, this generation just dropped it.

GIFTS

First girl: Weren't you kind of nervous when your boyfriend gave you all those beautiful gifts?
Second girl: No. I just kept calm and collected.

GINGER

Mark: What is the name of your dog?
Ryan: Ginger.
Mark: Does Ginger bite?
Ryan: No, but Ginger snaps.

GLACIERS

A lady on her first visit to Yellowstone National Park said to her guide, "Look at all those big rocks. Wherever did they come from?"

"The glaciers brought them down," said the guide.

"But where are the glaciers?"

"The glaciers," said the guide in a weary voice, "have gone back for more rocks."

GLARE

Matt: Did you see that conductor? He glared at me as if I hadn't paid my fare.
Pat: And what did you do?
Matt: I glared right back as if I had.

GLUE

Speaker: Yes, my audiences are glued to their seats when I speak.

Bored listener: What a quaint way of keeping them there.

GNU

Mama Gnu To Papa Gnu: I want you to punish our little one. He has been bad all day.

Papa Gnu: No, I won't punish him. You will have to paddle your own gnu.

GOLF

Two men were beginning a game of golf. The first man stepped to the tee, and his first drive gave him a hole-in-one. The second man stepped up to the tee and said, "Okay, now I'll take my practice swing, and then we'll start the game."

* * *

First golfer: What's your golf score?

Second golfer: Well, not so good. It's 72.

First golfer: That's not so bad. In fact, it's really good.

Second golfer: Well, I'm hoping I do better on the next hole.

* * *

I shoot my golf game in the low 70's. When it gets any colder, I quit.

*   *   *

Lady customer: I would like to buy a low handicap.
Sales clerk at sporting goods shop: A low handicap? I don't understand.
Lady customer: I want to give it to my husband for his birthday, he's always wishing for one.

*   *   *

Yes, it is true. We have more golf curses per mile than anywhere else in the world.

*   *   *

There was once a Scotchman who had played golf with the same ball for 30 years. One day he lost it and was forced to buy another. He walked into the local sports shop and said, "Well, here I am again."

GOOD-BYE

Gabby woman leaving party: There was something I wanted to say before leaving, but I can't recall it just now.
Tired husband: Maybe it was good-bye.

GOOD LUCK

Bart: Did you hear what happened to the scientist who mixed poison ivy and a four-leaf clover?

Art: What happened?

Bart: He ended up with a rash of good luck.

GOOD NEWS/BAD NEWS

Agent to writer: I've got some good news and some bad news.

Writer: First tell me the good news.

Agent: Paramount just loved your story, absolutely ate it up.

Writer: That's fantastic, And the bad news?

Agent: Paramount is my dog.

* * *

The soldiers had been on the battlefield for weeks when the sergeant made an announcement.

"Men. I have some good news and some bad news for you. First the good news: Everyone will receive a change of socks. And now for the bad news. Walters, you will change with Hanson...Hanson you will change with Douglas...Douglas you will change with Kroeker...Kroeker you will change with Pedillia... Pedillia..."

* * *

Doctor: Would you like the good news or the bad news?

Patient: Give me the good news.

Doctor: You've only got three weeks to live.

Patient: If that's the good news, what's the bad news?
Doctor: I should have told you two weeks ago.

GOTCHA

The chief executive of a large corporation, who was a stickler for efficiency, made an inspection tour of one of the company's manufacturing units. As he led his subordinates from department to department, he was as proud as a peacock as the machines hummed and the men worked swiftly and efficiently.

Suddenly the executive heard some whistling from behind a stack of boxes. He confronted the whistler who was lying down on some of the boxes.

"What is your salary?" demanded the chief executive.

"Who me?" said the whistler.

"Yes, you."

"I make $100 a week," replied the young man as he continued whistling.

The chief executive was furious. He turned to one of his aides and said, "Give this young man $100 and get him out of here at once."

One of the courageous assistants said, "But C.J., he..."

"You heard me, $100 and move him out now."

Later that day the accounting department called the chief executive about the whistler.

"What account should we charge the $100 to, C.J.?"

"Payroll, naturally," said the executive with a huff.

"But C.J., that boy didn't work for us. He was a messenger waiting for a delivery receipt."

GOUT

A local minister was troubled by one of his members who was constantly drinking alcohol. They happened to run into each other at a shopping mall. The drinker came up to the minister and asked, "Pastor, what causes gout?"

The minister thought that this would be a good opportunity to admonish the man about his drinking. "It comes from drinking too much alcohol."

"Oh, I see," said the man. "I just read in the paper that the pope and the president were both suffering from gout."

GRAMMAR

Door-to-door salesman: Are your parents in, little girl?

Little girl: They was, but they's out now.

Salesman: Tsk, Tsk. Where's your grammar?

Little girl: She's in the kitchen baking bread.

GUILTY

Judge: Guilty or not guilty?

Prisoner: Not guilty.

Judge: Have you ever been to prison before?

Prisoner: No, this is the first time I have stolen anything.

*   *   *

Judge: You say you have known this man all your life. Do you think he would be guilty of stealing this money?

Witness: How much was it?

* * *

Judge: Guilty or not guilty?

Prisoner: Well, I thought I was guilty, but I've been talking to my lawyer and he's convinced me I'm not guilty.

GYMNASIUM

Lady at the store: I am a physical education teacher and I would like to buy a pair of shorts to wear around my gymnasium.

Clerk: Well, how big is your gymnasium?

HANDBAG

"I've stopped going to the psychiatrist. He told me this morning that I was in love with my handbag."

"That's ridiculous!"

"I know. I mean, we're very fond of each other, but love?"

HAMBURGER

Customer: What is the price of hamburger?

Butcher: One dollar and forty cents a pound.

Customer: One dollar and forty cents! The store down the street sells it for one dollar and fifteen cents a pound.

Butcher: Why don't you go there to shop?
Customer: I did, but they are all out of hamburger.
Butcher: Well, when I am out of hamburger, I sell it for a dollar a pound.

HAT

Husband: You call that a hat! My dear, I shall never stop laughing.
Wife: Oh, yes, you will. The bill will probably arrive tomorrow.

* * *

First man: I felt sorry for your wife in church this morning when she had a terrible attack of coughing and everyone turned to look at her.
Second man: You don't need to worry about that. She was wearing a new spring hat and dress.

HEADACHE

Mother: Doctor, doctor! My little Billy swallowed a dozen aspirin. What should I do?
Doctor: Are you sure it was a dozen?
Mother: Absolutely! Doctor, I'm scared to death.
Doctor: Calm down. Is little Billy crying?
Mother: No. Doctor: Is he sleeping?
Mother: No.
Doctor: Is his color funny?
Mother: No.

Doctor: Did he throw up?

Mother: No. But I'm scared. All that aspirin—shouldn't I do something?

Doctor: Try and give him a headache.

* * *

Dan: What does your mother do for a headache?

Stan: She sends me out to play.

* * *

Have you heard about the amazing new discovery? It's a pill that is half aspirin and half glue for people who have splitting headaches.

HEADS OR TAILS

The soles of my shoes are so thin I can step on a dime and tell whether it's heads or tails.

HEARING AID

Mark: I just purchased the most expensive hearing aid ever made. It is imported from Germany and is guaranteed for life.

Clark: How much did it cost?

Mark: Five past two.

HEART FAILURE

Teacher: Johnny, if your father earned $100 a week and gave your mother half, what would she have?

Johnny: Heart failure.

HEARTY MEAL

A minister went to visit some members of his church who owned a small farm. Before leaving for the morning service, the members invited him for breakfast. He declined saying that he found he did not preach well following a hearty meal.

When the members returned home after the morning services, the wife said to the husband, "He might as well have et."

HECKLER

"A horse! A horse! My kingdom for a horse," spoke the actor dramatically from the stage.

"Would a jackass do?" called out a heckler in the balcony.

"Why yes," said the actor. "Come on down."

HELL

An American tourist was looking down the crater of a large volcano in Greece and said, "It looks like hell."

The Greek guide responded, "You Americans have been everywhere."

HELLO

Q. What did the policeman say to the man with three heads?

A. Hello, hello, hello.

HITLER

At one point Hitler thought so much of himself that he ordered the government printing office to issue a stamp bearing his likeness. After a period of time the postal carriers began complaining that the stamps were falling off the envelopes. Every day their bags would be full of stamps.

Hitler paid a visit to the printers. He demanded to know why the highest grade of glue hadn't been used on his commemorative stamp.

"Oh, but it was," the trembling printer assured him. "We've looked into this unfortunate situation, and the problem, sir, is that the people are spitting on the wrong side."

HOBBIES

Ken: Have you ever had any hobbies?
Len: Let's see. I've had rheumatism and hives, and mumps—but I can't remember ever having hobbies.

DO YOUR HOMEWORK

Boy: Mama, why doesn't papa have any hair?
Mother: Because he thinks so much, dear.
Boy: Why do you have much, mama?
Mother: Because—oh, go do your homework.

HONORABLE

The judge was cross-examining a colonel. Unable to shake his testimony he tried sarcasm. "They call you colonel. In what regiment are you a colonel?" "Well," drawled the colonel, "It's like this. The 'Colonel' in front of my name is like the 'Honorable' in front of yours. It doesn't mean a thing."

HOW MANY WHEELS?

Husband: That man is really stupid.
Wife: Why do you say that?
Husband: He thinks that a football coach has four wheels.
Wife: Isn't that silly. How many wheels does it have?

HOW OLD

Son: Dad, how soon will I be old enough to do as I please?
Father: I don't know. Nobody has lived that long yet.

HOW'S THAT?

"Our paper is two days late this week," wrote an Idaho newspaper editor, "owing to an accident. When we started to run the press Monday night, one of the guy ropes gave way, allowing the forward glider fluke to fall and break as it struck the flunker flopper. This, of course, as anyone who knows anything about a press will readily understand, left the gangplank with only the flip-flap to support it, which also dropped and broke off the wooper-cock. This loosened the fluking between the ramrod and the flibber-snatcher, which caused trouble with the mogus.

"The report that the delay was caused by our over-indulgence in stimulants is a tissue of falsehoods. The redness in the appearance of our right eyes was caused by our going into the hatchway of the press in our anxiety to start it, and pulling the coppling pin after the slap-bang was broken, which caused the dingus to rise up and welt us in the optic. We expect a brand new glider fluke on this afternoon's train."

HUNCH

Willy: I had a hunch today. I got up at seven, had seven dollars in my pocket, there were seven people at lunch, and there were seven horses in the race. I picked the seventh horse to win.

Billy: So he came in the winner?

Willy: No, he came in seventh.

HUSBANDS

All husbands are alike, but they have different faces so that women can tell them apart.

IDEA

Student: I've just had a brilliant idea.
Teacher: It's probably beginner's luck.

IDLE

"He is the idol of the family."
"Yes, he has been idle for 20 years."

IMPERSONATION

Father: Did you reprimand Walter for mimicking me?
Mother: Yes, I told him not to act like a fool.

IMPRESSIONIST

A man walked into a theatrical agent's office, stood on a chair, flapped his arms, and flew twice around the room before landing on the agent's desk.

"How about that?" he said.

"Sorry," said the agent. "There's no demand for bird impressionists these days."

INFANTRY

Q. What's the youngest branch in the Army?
A. The infantry.

INJURED

"I was injured on the football team."
"How?"
"I fell off the bench."

INSANE

Judge: Gentlemen of the jury, have you come to a decision?

Foreman: We have, Your Honor. The jury is all of the same mind—temporarily insane.

* * *

Visitor: Why are you here?

Insane patient: For no reason at all.

* * *

Husband: My wife talks to herself—she must be insane.

Psychiatrist: Ridiculous. You wouldn't be insane just because you talked to yourself.

Husband: No?

Psychiatrist: Of course not. I talk to myself. Do you think I'm insane?

Husband: I wouldn't say you're insane if you talked to yourself. But you would be if you listened.

INSECTS

"This is an ideal spot for a picnic."

"It must be. Fifty-million insects can't be wrong."

INSURANCE

A farmer whose barn burned down was told by the insurance company that his policy provided that the company build a new barn, rather than paying him the cash value. The farmer was incensed by this. "If that is the way you fellows operate," he said, "then cancel the insurance I have on my wife's life."

* * *

To illustrate how swiftly life insurance claims are paid, one salesman said that his company's offices were on the 10th floor of a 60-floor skyscraper, and that one day a man fell off the roof and was handed his check as he passed their floor.

INTERVIEW

Politician: I have nothing to say to the newspaper.
Reporter: I know that. Now let's get down to the interview.

INVALID

"I was an invalid once."
"You were? When was that?"
"When I was a baby. I couldn't walk until I was a year old."

INVENTOR

The most famous Irish inventor was Pat Pending.

I REMEMBER

Father: When I was your age, I was up at five every morning. I fed the chickens, cleared the snow from around the house, and then did my six-mile paper route. And I thought nothing of it.

Son: I don't blame you, Dad. I don't think much of it, either.

IRS

Q. What do you need when you have an IRS auditor buried to his neck in concrete?

A. More concrete.

*   *   *

Someday the income tax return will be simplified to: How much money have you got? Where is it? When can you get it?

*   *   *

The three R's of the IRS: This is ours, that is ours, everything is ours.

JEWELS

A woman making arrangements with an artist to sit for her portrait said to him, "Although I have only a few items of jewelry, nevertheless I want this painting to show me wearing diamond rings and earrings, an emerald brooch, and a multistrand necklace of pearls that look like they are priceless."

"I can do this all right," said the artist. "But do you mind telling me why you want this, when apparently you do not particularly care for jewelry?"

"You see, if I die first," said the woman, "and my husband marries again, I want that second wife to go out of her mind trying to find out where he hid the jewels."

JOB

"My brother's got a job in an electric shop. One day he grabbed hold of a live wire."

"What happened?"

"I don't know—but it's the only job he ever held on to."

JOKES

Dan: How do you like my jokes?

Stan: I can't see anything funny in them.

Dan: Oh well, you'll probably catch on after a while and laugh.

Stan: No, I laughed at them 20 years ago.

*   *   *

"When I tell jokes people clap their hands."

"Yeah, clap them over their ears."

*   *   *

Gary: So you didn't like my jokes.

Harry: No, they were terrible.

Gary: Oh, I don't know about that—I threw a bunch of them in the furnace and the fire roared.

JOY

Lady: Young man, I am going to give you a quarter not because you deserve it, but because it pleases me to do so.

Beggar: Thanks, but why not make it a dollar so you can really enjoy yourself?

JERK

While reading the newspaper, Walter came across an article about a beautiful actress and model who married a boxer who was not noted for his IQ.

"I'll never understand," he said to his wife, "why the biggest jerks get the most attractive wives."

His wife replied, "Why, thank you, dear."

JUDGMENT

Husband: You must admit, that men have better judgment than women.

Wife: Oh, yes. You married me, and I married you.

JUSTICE

A Chinese description of American court trials: "One man is silent, another talks all the time, and 12 wise men condemn the man who has not said a word."

KAYAK

Did you hear about the Eskimo who put some oil heaters in his kayak and was surprised when they exploded and set fire to it. Which only goes to prove that you can't have your kayak and heat it, too.

KING OF SIAM

Rich: I once sang for the King of Siam. At least that's what he told me he was.

Dave: Yes, he said, "If you're a singer, then I'm the King of Siam."

KNIT

"Did you know that it takes a dozen sheep to make a sweater?"

"Really. I didn't know they could knit!"

KNOWLEDGE

Before marriage a man declares that he will be the boss in his home or know the reason why; after marriage he knows the reason why.

LADDER

Pam: I fell off a sixty-foot ladder today.

Melba: It's a miracle you weren't killed.

Pam: Oh, I only fell off the first rung.

LAMPPOST

First Russian: In America the people are so honest, you can hang your watch on a lamppost and come back in three weeks and it's still there.

Second Russian: You mean to say that in America you can hang your watch on a lamppost and come back in three weeks and your watch is still there?

First Russian: No, the lamppost is still there.

LARK

Joe: I spent ten dollars on a canary yesterday.

Moe: That's nothing. I spent fifty on a lark.

LAST WORDS

Doctor: Do you remember what your husband's last words were?

Wife: Oh yes. He said, "I wonder how they can make a profit selling this red salmon at fifteen cents a can?"

LATE

Boss: What's the idea of coming in here late every morning?

Employee: It's your fault. You have trained me so thoroughly not to watch the clock in the office, now I'm in the habit of not looking at it at home.

LAWSUIT

Son: Papa! Papa! The lid to our coal-shoot was left open and a man fell down inside. What should I do?

Father: Quick! Put the cover on it. I'll call a cop and have him arrested before he can sue us.

LAWYERS

Lawyers can compress the most words into the smallest ideas better than anyone I have ever met.

*   *   *

Brenda: My dad wanted to be a lawyer badly.
Sharon: Are there any other kind of lawyers except bad ones?

*   *   *

Do you know the difference between a dead chicken in the road and a dead lawyer in the road? There are skid marks in front of the chicken.

*   *   *

Do you know why they bury lawyers sixteen feet deep in the ground? Because lawyers are real good down deep.

*   *   *

Did you hear about the man who was walking through a graveyard and noticed a grave stone that said, HERE LIES A LAWYER AND A GOOD MAN. "Imagine that," said the man to himself, "two men buried in the same grave."

*   *   *

Did you hear the good news and the bad news? The good news is that a bus load of lawyers just ran off the cliff. The bad news is that there was three empty seats on the bus.

*   *   *

A lawyer is a man who gets two other men to strip for a fight and then takes their clothes.

*   *   *

"I'm looking for a criminal lawyer. Have you one here?"
"Well, we think we have, but we can't prove it yet."

*   *   *

"What do you have when you have 20,000 lawyers at the bottom of the ocean?"
"You have a good start."

*   *   *

"What is wrong when you have a lawyer buried up to his neck in the sand?"
"You don't have enough sand."

*   *   *

A burglar's wife was being cross-examined by the district attorney.
Attorney: Are you the wife of this prisoner?
Woman: Yes.

Attorney: You knew he was a burglar when you married him?

Woman: Yes.

Attorney: May I ask how you came to marry such an individual?

Woman: You may. You see I was getting older and had to choose between marrying a burglar or a lawyer.

* * *

Lawyer: Are you positive that the prisoner is the man who stole your car?

Witness: Well, I was until you cross-examined me. Now I'm not sure whether I ever had a car at all.

* * *

Judge: Have you anything to offer the court before sentence is passed upon you?

Prisoner: No, Your Honor. My lawyer took my last dollar.

* * *

Lawyer: Seventy-five dollars, please.

Client: What for?

Lawyer: My advice.

Client: I'm not taking it.

* * *

Crook: I got nearly a million in cash in my bank box. Can you get me off?

Lawyer: Believe me, pal, you'll never go to prison with that kind of money.

And sure enough, he did not. He went to prison flat broke.

* * *

Lawyer: When did the robbery take place?

Witness: I think...

Lawyer: We don't care what you think, sir. We want to know what you know.

Witness: Then if you don't want to know what I think, I might as well leave the stand. I can't talk without thinking. I'm no lawyer.

* * *

One day the gate between Heaven and Hell broke down, and Saint Peter and Satan got into a bitter dispute about whose responsibility it was to repair it. After much argument they could not arrive at an agreement. Then Saint Peter said he would hire a lawyer to defend the interests of Heaven.

"Where are you going to get a lawyer?" asked Satan. "I've got them all."

* * *

Lawyer: Now repeat to the court, word-for-word, what the defendant said.

Witness: I'd rather not. They're not words fit to tell a gentleman.

Lawyer: In that case, lean over and whisper them in my ear.

* * *

A lawyer had successfully handled a difficult law case for a wealthy friend. Following the happy outcome of the case, the friend and client called on the lawyer, expressed his appreciation of his work, and handed him a handsome Moroccan leather wallet.

The lawyer looked at the wallet in astonishment and handed it back with a sharp reminder that a wallet could not possibly compensate him for his services. "My fee for that work," acidly snapped the attorney, "is 500 dollars."

The client opened the wallet, removed a 1,000 dollar bill, replaced it with a 500 dollar bill, and handed it back to the lawyer with a smile.

LAZY

The owner of a large ranch in Texas had 50 men working for him. None of them worked as hard as he expected them to work. One day he had an idea about how to cure his men of their laziness.

He called them together and said, "I've got a nice easy job for the laziest man on the ranch. Will the laziest man please step forward." Every man stepped forward except one man.

"Why didn't you step over with the rest of the men?" asked the rancher.

"Too much trouble," said the man.

LEFTOVERS

A preacher forgot his notes for the sermon he was going to deliver. In the midst of the sermon he got a few things twisted when he said that the Lord took 4000 barley loaves and 6000 fishes and fed 24 people, and had plenty left over.

Someone in the congregation called out, "Anybody could do that."

"Could you?" asked the minister.

"Certainly I could."

After the service, when the minister complained about the heckler's conduct, he was told of his error by a deacon.

"Well, next week I will not forget my notes. I'll fix that character."

The next week the minister stepped forward confidently and began his sermon. In the course of it, he brought up again the miracle of the loaves and fishes. He told how the five barley loaves and the two fishes had fed the multitude of probably 24,000 people. He then pointed to the heckler from the previous Sunday and asked, "Could you do that?"

"I sure could," said the heckler.

"And just how would you do that?" asked the minister.

"With the loaves and fishes leftover from last Sunday."

LIAR

The game warden was walking through the mountains when he encountered a hunter with a gun. "This is good territory for hunting, don't you think?" suggested the warden.

"You bet it is," said the hunter enthusiastically. "I killed one of the finest bucks yesterday—it weighed at least 250 pounds."

"Deer are out of season now," said the warden. "Do you know that you are talking to a game warden?"

"No, I was not aware of that," said the hunter. "And I'll bet you didn't know that you've been talking to the biggest liar in the state."

LICENSE

Two fellows out hunting were stopped by a game warden. One of them took off running and the game warden went after him and caught him. The fellow then showed the warden his hunting license.

"Why did you run when you had a license?"

"Because the other fellow didn't have one."

LIE

First wife: Does your husband lie awake all night?
Second wife: Yes, and he lies in his sleep, too.

LIE DETECTOR

First man: Have you ever seen one of those machines that can tell when a person is telling a lie?
Second man: Seen one? I married one!

LIGHT

Teacher: How fast does light travel?
Student: I'm not sure, but I do know it always gets here too early in the morning.

LILACS

Fan: You certainly sang "Lilacs in the Rain" beautifully. You sang the words so well I could smell the lilacs.

Singer: The words? What about my singing?

Fan: I could smell that, too.

LOAN

Larry: Lend me ten dollars.

Harry: I can't spare it.

Larry: All right, lend me ten dollars and give me five dollars now. Then I'll owe you five dollars and you'll owe me five dollars, and we'll call it square.

* * *

Stan: How about lending me $50?

Dan: Sorry, I can only let you have $25.

Stan: But why not the entire $50, Dan?

Dan: No, $25 only, that way it's even—each one of us loses $25.

* * *

"I think you're a nice kid. I've known you for about five years. Could you let me have five dollars?"

"I'm sorry—I couldn't."

"Why?"

"Because I have known you for five years."

* * *

Max: You couldn't loan me $20, could you?
Jeff: No, but how did you know it?

* * *

"Loan me ten dollars, will you?"
"No."
"I was only fooling."
"I wasn't."

* * *

"I'm looking for somebody to lend me $50."
"Well, you certainly have a nice day for it."

* * *

"Have you money for a cup of coffee, mister?"
"No, but don't worry about me, I'll get along all right."

* * *

"Hello, this is George."
"Hello, George. What's on your mind?"
"I'm broke down in Los Angeles and I need $200 right away."
"There must be something wrong with the line. I can't hear you."
"I say, I want to borrow $200."
"I can't hear a word you're saying."
Operator (coming on the line): "Hello! This is the operator. I can hear your party very plainly."
"Then you give him the $200."

LOOKOUT

In appearance, I'm not a great star,
Others are handsomer—far.
But my face—I don't mind it
Because I'm behind it;
It's the poor folks out front that I jar.

LOVE

Here's to love—the only fire for which there is no insurance.

LUNCH

"Shall I bring you lunch on deck, sir?"
"Just throw it overboard and save time."

MARRIAGE

"Time separates the best of friends."
"So does money."
"And don't forget marriage."

* * *

Ben: I think she married me for my money.
Len: Well, she earned it.

* * *

Before marriage a man thinks nothing is good enough for his wife. After marriage he still thinks nothing is good enough for her.

MARTIAN

A Martian wandered from his spaceship in the desert into Las Vegas and arrived when one of the slot machines was spewing forth a bunch of nickels. When the exploding gadget had subsided, the Martian went over to it and said, "With a cold like that, you ought to take some aspirin and get into bed."

MATCH

Writer: Can't you suggest something to put a finishing touch on my story?
Editor: Yes. A match.

MATH

Son to father: Remember, you promised me $20 if I passed math. Well, I've got great news. You've just saved $20.

MEMORY

Teacher: What was George Washington most famous for?
Student: His memory.
Teacher: That's an odd answer. What makes you think Washington's memory was so remarkable?
Student: Well, they sure put up a lot of monuments to it.

MESSY

First husband: Does your wife keep a messy home?
Second husband: Let's put it this way, when the toast pops out of the toaster, it takes an hour to find it.

MISTAKES

Boss: How can one person make so many mistakes in a single day?
Employee: I get up early.

MONDAY

Prisoner: You mean they're going to hang me?
Guard: Yes, on Monday morning.
Prisoner: Can't you hang me on Saturday?
Guard: Why don't you want to hang on Monday?
Prisoner: Well, it seems like a terrible way to start the week.

MONEY

Money isn't everything, and don't let anyone tell you different. There are other things, such as stocks, bonds, letters of credit, checks, traveler's checks, and drafts.

*   *   *

Money doesn't always bring happiness. A man with 20 million dollars isn't any happier than a man with 9 million dollars.

MOVIES

A mother and daughter were watching a 1930s film on TV. As it ended with the usual romantic clinch and fade-out of that era, the teenager said, "Gosh, Mom, your movies ended where ours begin."

MOTHER-IN-LAW

"My mother-in-law passed away last week."
"What was the complaint?"
"There was no complaint. Everybody was satisfied."

MOVING

First neighbor: We are going to move. We're going to be living in a better neighborhood.
Second neighbor: So are we.
First neighbor: Oh, are you also moving?
Second neighbor: No, we're staying right here.

MUD PIE

A distraught mother went to a psychiatrist and said that her son was always making mud pies, and when he had finished them he ate them.

"That's not too unusual," said the psychiatrist. "Lots of boys make mud pies and try to eat them."

"I'm not so sure of that," said the mother, "and neither is my son's wife."

MUGGING

Then there's the city where crime has gotten so bad that citizens figure muggings into their budgets.

MUSTACHE

Teacher: Can any bright pupil tell me why a man's hair turns gray before his mustache?

Student: Cause his hair has a twenty-year head start on his mustache.

*   *   *

Suzie: George's mustache made me laugh.

Jeanie: Yeah. It tickled me, too.

NAIL-BITING

"I finally made my son stop biting his nails."

"How did you manage to do that?"

"I made him wear shoes."

NAIL POLISH

Q. What would you use to shine a screw?
A. Nail polish.

NAME

If you are looking for a name for a new pet try one of these.

A white mouse	Mousey Tung
A Collie	Flower
A Collie	Melon
A Boxer	Shorts
A rabbit	Transit
A donkey	Shane
A pigeon	Toad
A frog...............	Horn
A horse.............	Greeley
A rooster	Shire Sos
A gopher	Broke
A crow	Magnon
A sparrow	Agnew
A kitten	Kaboodle
A cat................	Mandu
A rat................	Frank Lloyd
A rat................	Fink

NAMES

Lady of the house: I want you to stand at the front door and call the guests' names as they arrive.

Butler: Very well, madam. I've been wanting to do that for years.

NECKING

The dean of women at a large coeducational college posted an announcement that started with the sentence: The president of the college and I have decided to stop necking on the campus.

NEW ORLEANS

A number of children from the neighborhood were invited to Mrs. Johnson's for a Thanksgiving dinner. She decided to do something different while serving the meal.

"Where are you originally from?"

"California," said the boy.

"Well then, I will give you the left wing."

She turned to another boy.

"Where are you from?"

"New York," he answered.

"You get the right wing."

She turned to the third boy.

"Where are you from?"

"I'm from New Orleans and I ain't hungry."

NERVOUS

A local minister was asked to speak for a ladies auxiliary meeting at a downtown hotel. He was reviewing his speech and was pacing back and forth across the room.

Suddenly he was interrupted by a woman who asked, "Are you nervous about speaking to the ladies auxiliary?"

"Me, nervous? Not a bit. I'm used to speaking to groups."

"In that case," asked the lady, "what are you doing here in the ladies room?"

NINE

Teacher: If two's company and three's a crowd, what are four and five?
Student: Nine.

NOAH

Sunday school teacher: How could Noah see in the dark?
Student: He had floodlighting on the ark.

NOODLE SOUP

Customer: Yes, I know that fish is brain-food. But I don't care much for fish. Isn't there some other kind of brain-food?
Waiter: Well, there's noodle soup.

NUTS

There are more men than women in mental institutions—which goes to show who's driving who nuts.

NUTS TO YOU

A pastor got this note accompanying a box of goodies, addressed to him and his wife from an elderly lady in the church.

Dear Pastor,

Knowing that you do not eat sweets, I am sending the candy to your wife—and nuts to you.

ODD

First boy: My dad is an Odd Fellow.
Second boy: Your mother is quite a peculiar character, also.

OFFERING

A minister was just about ready to go into the church for the morning service, when he discovered that he could not find the offering plates. He informed the chairman of the Board of Deacons.

"I can't find the offering plates. I have to start the

service now. See if you can find something to collect the offering in."

The chairman of the Board of Deacons searched for something to collect the offering in. He could not find any plates, bags, or even boxes. He thought about someone's shoe, but dismissed that as not being too dignified.

When the time came for the offering, four ushers walked down the aisle wearing broad grins and carrying shiny receptacles. The chairman had resourcefully borrowed four hubcaps from a car in the parking lot.

OHIO

Teacher: Who discovered America?

Student: Ohio.

Teacher: Ohio? That's ridiculous. It was Columbus.

Student: Yes, sir. I know. But I didn't think it was necessary to mention the gentleman's first name, sir.

OLD AGE

Patient: How can I live to be a hundred, Doctor?

Doctor: Give up cookies, cake, and ice cream. Stop eating red meat, potatoes, and bread. And no soft drinks.

Patient: And if I do that, I will live to be a hundred?

Doctor: Maybe not, but it will certainly seem like it.

OLD BOSSY

A man's car stopped dead as he was driving along an old country road. He got out of his car, lifted the hood, and looked at the motor. Just then, a big black and white cow came along and stopped beside him. The cow also looked under the hood at the motor.

"Your trouble is probably the carburetor," said the cow.

The startled man jumped back and ran down the road until he met a farmer. He told the farmer what had happened.

The farmer asked, "Was the cow black and white?"

"Yes, yes!" cried the motorist.

"Oh, don't pay attention to Old Bossy. She doesn't know a thing about cars."

OLD CAR

Willy: Why did you bury your old car?

Billy: Well, the battery was dead, the pistons were shot, and then the engine died.

ONE FOOT

Some speakers and most listeners would approve of the rule among certain tribes in Africa. Their regulation is that when a man rises to speak he must stand on one foot while delivering his speech. The minute the lifted foot touches the ground, the speech ends—or the speaker is forcibly silenced.

ONE LESS

Husband: Well, we have a tremendous party planned for tonight. I wonder how many truly great men will be here?

Wife: There will be one less than you think.

OOPS

One winter evening a motorcycle driver reversed his jacket so that the bitter winds would not come through the gaps between the buttons. As he sped along the road, he skidded on an icy spot and crashed into a tree.

When the ambulance arrived, the first-aid man pushed through the crowd and asked a man who was standing over the victim what happened. He replied that the motorcycle rider seemed to be in pretty good shape after the crash, but by the time they got his head straightened out he was dead.

*　　*　　*

First man: Who is that awful-looking lady in the corner?

Second man: Why, that's my wife.

First man: Oh, I don't mean her (trying to get out of the situation), I mean the lady next to her.

Second man: That is my daughter.

OPERA

Wife: Did you notice how the opera singer's voice filled the hall?

Husband: Yes. I also noticed that a lot of people left to make room for it.

OPINION

Writer: What do you think of my joke book? Give me your honest opinion.

Editor: It isn't worth anything.

Writer: I know, but give it to me anyway.

OPPORTUNITY

"May I ask you the secret of your success?"

"There is no easy street. You just jump at your opportunity."

"But how can I tell when my opportunity comes?"

"You can't. You've got to keep on jumping."

ORANGES

Customer: Three of those oranges you sent me were rotten. I'll bring them back.

Merchant: That's all right, you needn't bring them back. Your word is just as good as the oranges.

OURS

Wife: And another thing I want to tell you. I've noticed every time you talk, you say my house, my automobile, my chair, my shoes—everything's yours. You never say ours. I'm your partner. I'm your wife. It should be ours.

The husband paid no attention to his wife and just kept looking around the room for something.

Wife: What are you looking for?

Husband: Our pants.

PAL

Dave: I'll never forget the time we were ice skating on the lake. Suddenly the ice broke and I plunged into the water. You threw off your coat and shoes, and jumped in after me. What a pal.

Walter: What do mean pal? Why wouldn't I jump in after you? You had my jacket and skates on.

PANTS

Pants are made for men and not for women. Women are made for men and not for pants. When a man pants for a woman and a woman pants for a man, that makes a pair of pants. Pants are like molasses, they are thinner in hot weather and thicker in cold weather. There has been much discussion as to whether pants is singular or plural; but it seems to us that when men wear pants it's plural, and when they don't, it's singular. If you want to make the pants last, make the coat first.

*   *   *

Kenny: I just bought a new suit with two pairs of pants.
Lenny: Well, how do you like it?
Kenny: Fine, only it's too hot wearing two pairs.

PASTOR

Frances: What do you think of our new pastor?
Sharon: On six days of the week he is invisible, and on the seventh day he is incomprehensible.

PATIENCE

The world would be a better place if all men showed as much patience as they do when they're waiting for a fish to bite.

PAY OFF

Salesman: Believe me, this sewing machine will pay for itself in no time.
Customer: Good. When it does, send it to me.

PEARLY GATES

A minister and a congressman arrived at the pearly gates. Saint Peter greeted both of them and gave them their room assignments.

"Pastor, here are the keys to one of our nicest efficiency units. And for you, Mr. Congressman, the keys to our finest penthouse suite."

"What is the deal?" asked the minister. "This is unfair!"

"Listen," said Saint Peter, "ministers are a dime a dozen up here, but this is the first congressman we've ever seen."

PENICILLIN

The best present for a man who's got everything is penicillin.

PERFECT PAIR

Husband: Nancy and Mike make a perfect pair, don't you think?

Wife: Yes. He's a pill and she's a headache.

PHONE

Teacher: If you weigh 150 pounds and you sit in the bath, what happens?

Student: The phone rings.

PIANO

Mark: My brother has been playing the piano for three years.

Clark: Aren't his fingers tired?

PICK

First husband: Does your wife select your clothes?

Second husband: No, but she picks my pockets.

PICKY, PICKY

Diner: Waiter, I want some oysters, but not too large or too small, too old or too tough, and they musn't be salty. I want them cold and I want them at once.

Waiter: Yes, sir. With or without pearls?

PIGEON-TOWED

There was once a beautiful fairy who yearned to be a ballet dancer. When she heard that the Royal Ballet was holding auditions in a nearby town, she harnessed 100 white pigeons to her chariot and flew to the theater. The director took one look at her spectacular entrance and told her to go away.

"But why?" she wailed.

"Because I've got enough pigeon-towed dancers in the company already."

PIGS

A city family decided to spend their vacation on a farm for the experience. The only thing they did not like was the noise that the pigs made.

The father wrote to the farmer the next year about coming again for another vacation. He asked if the pigs were still there. He received the following note from the farmer.

"Don't worry. We haven't had pigs on the farm since you were here."

*　　*　　*

"Do you know anything about pigs?"

"My father raised a big hog once."

"You're telling me."

PINCHING

"It's happened," cried the bishop in anguish as he sat playing bridge one evening with some charming people.

"What's happened?" asked the young woman next to him.

"A stroke: My left side is paralyzed."

"Are you sure?" asked the young lady.

"Yes, yes," groaned the bishop. "I've been pinching my left leg for the past few minutes and feel no sensation whatsoever."

"Relax," said the young lady. "That was my leg you were pinching."

PINS

Mark Twain said that when he was young he was impressed by the story of a young man who landed a job when the employer saw him pick up several pins from the sidewalk outside the firm's office.

So Twain went to the street alongside the office windows of a firm he wanted to work for and began almost ostentatiously to pick up pins he had earlier placed on the sidewalk. After a good number of pins had been picked up, a clerk came out and said, "The boss asked me to tell you to move along. Your idiotic behavior is distracting the people working in the office."

PITCHFORK

In defending a client charged with assault, a lawyer told the jury his client was walking down the road with a pitchfork on his shoulder. A large dog who was very fierce attacked the man, and the man killed the dog with the pitchfork.

"Why did you kill my dog?" demanded the dog's owner.

"Because he tried to bite me."

"But why did you not go at him with the other end of the pitchfork?"

"Why didn't your dog come at me with his other end?"

PLANE

Customer: Where is your plane?
Pilot: Over there—the tri-motor plane.
Customer: What do you mean tri-motor plane?
Pilot: If one motor goes bad, we'll try the other.

PLANTS

Wife: Plants grow faster if you talk to them.

Husband: But I don't know how to speak Geranium.

PLEASURE

First employee: Are you going to the boss' funeral?
Second employee: Oh, no, I'm working today. My motto is business before pleasure.

PLUM

Q. How do you tell a plum from an elephant?
A. A plum always forgets.

PLUMBER

Husband: Who put that statue under the sink?
Wife: That's no statue, that's the plumber.

POLITICIAN

The deaths of politicians should always appear under the public improvement section of the newspaper.

*   *   *

An honest politician is one who, when he is bought, will stay bought.

POLITICS

Minister: Before I vote and support you for sheriff, I'd like to know if you partake of intoxicating beverages.

Candidate for sheriff: Before I answer, tell me if this is an inquiry or an invitation?

*　　*　　*

Politics is the art of looking for trouble, finding it everywhere, diagnosing it wrongly, and applying unsuitable remedies.

POSTCARD

The following postcard was received.

Dear George,

We both miss you as much as if you were right here.

POSTDATED

A motorist driving by a Texas ranch hit and killed a calf that was crossing the road. The driver went to the owner of the calf, and explained what had happened. He then asked what the animal was worth.

"Oh about $200 today." said the rancher. "But in six years it would have been worth $900. So $900 is what I'm out."

The motorist sat down and wrote out a check and handed it to the farmer.

"Here," he said, "is the check for $900. It is post-dated six years from now."

POTATOES

Q. Why did the potatoes argue all the time?
A. They couldn't see eye-to-eye about anything.

POULTRY

Employee: Aren't you ashamed to give me such a poultry paycheck?
Boss: You mean paltry.
Employee: No, I mean poultry. It's chicken feed.

PRACTICAL

City slicker: Is it right to say "a hen lays" or "a hen lies eggs?"
Farmer: Where I come from, the people just lift her up to see.

PRAYER

Noticing that just before the football game started both teams gathered together and prayed briefly, a fan, seated next to a minister, asked what he thought would happen if both teams prayed with equal faith and fervor.

"In that event," replied the minister, "I imagine the Lord would simply sit back and enjoy one fine game of football."

PREGNANT

The rather awkward freshman at a prom finally got up enough nerve to ask a sultry young beauty for a dance. "I never dance with a child," said the pretty little snob.

The freshman looked her over critically and said, "Please forgive me; I didn't realize you were pregnant."

*　　*　　*

An obviously pregnant woman was asked by another woman, "Are you going to have a baby?"

"Oh, no," replied the mother-to-be, "I'm just carrying this for a friend."

PRESIDENT

A man walked up to the desk of a resort hotel and asked for a room.

"Have you a reservation?" asked the indifferent clerk.

"No. But I've been coming here every year for 12 years, and I've never had to have a reservation."

"Well, there is nothing available. We are filled up, and without a reservation you can't get a room."

"Suppose the president of the United States came in. You would have a room for him, wouldn't you?"

"Of course, for the president we would find a room—we would have a room."

"All right," said the man. "Now I'm telling you that the president isn't coming here tonight. So give me his room."

PROFIT

Q. What kind of money do fishermen make?
A. Net profits.

PROPOSAL

Girl one: I did not accept Jeff the first time he proposed.

Girl two: Of course not, my dear. You were not there.

PSYCHIATRIST

Patient: I'm dead.

Psychiatrist: That's impossible. You are talking to me right now.

Patient: I'm dead.

Psychiatrist: Now stand in front of that mirror and say, "Dead men don't bleed," for the next three hours.

At the end of that time the psychiatrist pricked the man's finger with a needle and it began to bleed.

Psychiatrist: There now, what does that prove?

Patient: Dead men do bleed.

*   *   *

Patient: Doctor, I get the feeling that people don't give a hoot about anything I say.

Psychiatrist: So?

*   *   *

Wife: You have got to help me, doctor. My husband keeps going around the house emptying ashtrays. He even does it in public places. I can't stand it!

Psychiatrist: That's not at all unusual, lots of people empty ashtrays.

Wife: Into their mouths?

*   *   *

Psychiatrist: I have treated you for six months and now you are cured. You will no longer have delusions of grandeur and imagine that you're Napoleon.

Patient: That's wonderful. I can hardly wait to go home and tell Josephine the good news.

PUNISH

Student: Would you punish someone for something they didn't do?

Teacher: Of course not.

Student: Good, 'cause I haven't done my homework.

PUNISHMENT

Then there was the author who suffered from writer's cramp—also known as authoritis.

*   *   *

Husband: Listen to this. This article states that in some of the old Roman prisons that have been unearthed, they found the petrified remains of the prisoners.

Wife: Gracious! Those must be what they call hardened criminals.

*　　*　　*

Joe: What would a cannibal be if he ate his mother's sister?

Moe: I give up.

Joe: An aunteater.

*　　*　　*

Pete: Do you know who owned the smallest radio in the world?

Bill: No, who?

Pete: Paul Revere—he broadcast from one plug.

*　　*　　*

"I want to have my face on some money."

"I would be glad if I had my hands on some."

*　　*　　*

"A little bird told me."

"It must have been a stool pigeon."

*　　*　　*

Dan: I'm named after my parents. My dad's name was Ferdinand and my mother's name was Liza.

Stan: What's your name, then?
Dan: Ferdiliza.

*   *   *

"A man dropped off the eaves of this building and was killed."
"That's what he deserves for eavesdropping."

*   *   *

Needless to say, one of the most successful inventors of all time was the man who invented a hay-baling machine. He made a bundle.

*   *   *

The next most successful man was the chemist who created a lubricant for furniture wheels. He called it caster oil.

*   *   *

There was also the two very competitive silkworms who had a race. It ended in a tie.

*   *   *

"He spilled rum on his whiskers and when lighting his cigarette his whiskers caught on fire."
"What did he do then?"
"Oh, he just fiddled with his whiskers while rum burned."

*   *   *

Gary: A man just sold me the Nile River.
Larry: Egypt you.

* * *

Did you hear about the man who swallowed an unplucked goose? He felt a little down in the mouth.

* * *

Mark: Did you hear about the billboard on the side of the road? It was owned by an old man called Lang.
Clark: No, I didn't.
Mark: Everybody called it old Lang's sign.

* * *

Did you hear about the fellow who spilled some root beer on the stove? Now he has foam on the range.

* * *

Lem: I just sat down on a pin.
Clem: Did it hurt?
Lem: No, it was a safety pin.

* * *

A man came into the bank to get a loan. He went up to the teller and said, "Who arranges for loans?"

"I'm sorry, sir," the teller told him, "but the loan arranger is out to lunch."

"All right," said the man. "May I speak to Tonto?"

* * *

Q. What do you call two fat men having a chat?
A. A heavy discussion.

* * *

Q. What lies on the ground 100 feet in the air?
A. A sunbathing centipede.

* * *

Q. How did Moses part the Red Sea?
A. With a sea saw.

* * *

Q. Why did the priest giggle?
A. Mass hysteria.

* * *

Q. What do you call great bodies of water filled with grape juice?
A. The Grape Lakes.

* * *

Q. What ballet do squirrels like?
A. The Nutcracker.

* * *

Q. What's a pig's favorite ballet?
A. Swine Lake.

* * *

Q. Which fly makes films?
A. Steven Spielbug.

*   *   *

Q. How do you make a glowworm happy?
A. Cut off its tail. It'll be delighted.

*   *   *

Q. What is sticky and plays the trumpet?
A. Gluey Armstrong.

*   *   *

Q. What did the German clock maker say to the broken clock?
A. Ve have vays of making you tock.

*   *   *

Q. What did the man do after his cat was run over by a steam roller?
A. He just sat there with a long puss.

*   *   *

Ryan: Did you hear about the dentist who married the manicurist?
Bryan: No, I didn't.
Ryan: It didn't last. After a month they were fighting tooth and nail.

*   *   *

Willy: That boat did 25 miles per hour.

Billy: Twenty-five miles? You mean knots.

Willy: Well, miles to me, knots to you.

*   *   *

Beggar: Sir, could you spare 20 dollars?

Man: Twenty dollars! What makes you think you can ask people for money like that?

Beggar: I just thought that it would be best to put all my begs in one ask it.

*   *   *

A tiger was walking through the jungle one day and saw two men relaxing under a tree. One was reading a newspaper, and the other was working feverishly on a manual typewriter.

The tiger leapt on the man with the newspaper, and ate him up. The tiger did not bother the other man at all. That's because any predator knows that readers digest but writers cramp.

*   *   *

One day a large elephant saw a turtle near a pond. The elephant lumbered over and squashed the turtle under its large foot.

A jackal who saw the murder ran over to the elephant and said, "Why did you do that?"

The elephant replied, "This is the same turtle that bit off the tip of my trunk 17 years ago, when I went to get a drink out of the river."

The jackal's eyes widened. "The same one? You must have an incredible memory!"

Raising its head proudly, the elephant said, "Turtle recall."

*   *   *

Unable to find a replacement cog for his car engine, a Datsun owner was told that he would have to go to Japan to get one.

He didn't want to make the trip for so little, so he decided to buy six-dozen cogs and bring them back to America and sell them, to help pay for the flight.

On the flight back, there was engine trouble and to save fuel the pilot gave orders to jettison all baggage. This meant that the cogs had to go also.

On the ground below, an elderly couple looked up at the sky. They saw all the baggage falling from the plane.

"Look, Sarah," said the old man. "It's raining Datsun cogs."

*   *   *

One day in the forest, three animals were discussing who among them was the most powerful.

"I am," said the hawk, "because I can fly and swoop down swiftly at my prey."

"That's nothing," said the mountain lion, "I am not only fleet, but I have powerful teeth and claws."

"I am the most powerful," said the skunk, "because with a flick of my tail, I can drive off the two of you."

Just then a huge grizzly bear lumbered out of the forest and settled the debate by eating them all... hawk, lion, and stinker.

QUESTIONS AND ANSWERS

Q. Where do armies live?
A. Up the sleevies of your jacket.

*　　*　　*

Q. What's a nun's favorite song?
A. I Left My Heart with San Franciscans.

*　　*　　*

Q. What's the best way to defeat your opponent?
A. Cut off his legs.

*　　*　　*

Q. What do they call a handsome, intelligent man in New York?
A. A tourist.

*　　*　　*

Q. What do you get if you cross a chicken with cement?
A. A bricklayer.

*　　*　　*

Q. What vegetable keeps the best musical rhythm?
A. The sugar beet.

*　　*　　*

Q. How do you keep an idiot waiting?
A. I'll tell you tomorrow.

*   *   *

Q. Why is it impossible to walk across Smogaria?
A. Nobody can hold his nose for that long.

*   *   *

Q. Where do fleas go in winter?
A. Search me.

*   *   *

Q. What will I do if I get seasick?
A. Don't worry—you'll do it.

*   *   *

Q. What is the best way to get to the emergency hospital?
A. Just stand out in the middle of the street.

*   *   *

Q. How did the accident happen?
A. My wife fell asleep in the backseat.

*   *   *

Q. How can you tell when salespeople are lying?
A. Their lips move.

*   *   *

Q. Do you know how Yuppies wean their children?
A. They fire the maid.

* * *

Q. What do sea monsters eat?
A. Fish and ships.

* * *

Q. What's green, bitter, and explodes?
A. A lime bomb.

* * *

Q. What is gray and stamps out jungle fires?
A. Smokey the elephant.

* * *

Q. Where does a sick ship go?
A. To the doc.

* * *

Q. What's black when it's clean, and white when it's dirty?
A. A blackboard.

* * *

Q. What do cars do at the disco?
A. Brake dance.

* * *

Q. What do fish sing to each other?
A. Salmon-chanted Evening.

*　　*　　*

Q. Where did the whale go when it was almost bankrupt?
A. He went to see the loan shark.

*　　*　　*

Q. Where did Noah keep the bees?
A. In the arkives.

*　　*　　*

Q. What do you get if you cross a hyena with a man-eating tiger?
A. I don't know, but if it laughs you'd better join in.

*　　*　　*

Q. Why do welders work such long hours?
A. Because they find their work so riveting.

*　　*　　*

Q. What is very quiet and explodes?
A. A mime bomb.

*　　*　　*

Q. What do you call a man who can't stop buying carpets?
A. A rug addict.

*　　*　　*

Q. How would you send a message to a shark?
A. Drop it a line.

*   *   *

Q. What did they call the canary that flew into the pastry dish?
A. Tweetie Pie.

*   *   *

Q. Who are all the fish of the sea afraid of?
A. Jack the Kipper.

*   *   *

Q. What's the largest thing ever made of grapes?
A. The Grape Wall of China.

*   *   *

Q. How does a monster count to 14?
A. On his fingers.

*   *   *

Q. Which famous comedian sacked Rome?
A. Attila the Fun.

*   *   *

Q. What goes woof, woof, tock?
A. A watchdog.

*   *   *

Q. How do you fix a broken tomato?
A. With tomato paste.

*   *   *

Q. What do cryogenicists sing when interring each new subject?
A. Freeze a Jolly Good Fellow.

*   *   *

Q. What's purple and surrounded by water?
A. Grape Britain.

*   *   *

Q. Why did the fig go out with a prune?
A. It couldn't find another date.

QUOTABLE QUOTES

Why doesn't the fellow who says, "I'm no speechmaker," let it go at that, instead of giving a demonstration.

*   *   *

Many can rise to the occasion, but few know when to sit down.

*   *   *

When it comes to spreading gossip, the female of the species is much faster than the mail.

*   *   *

Two feet on the ground are worth one in the mouth.

*   *   *

Yes, there are bigger things in life than money—bills, for instance.

*   *   *

Thrift is a wonderful virtue—especially in ancestors.

*   *   *

While money isn't everything in life, but it does keep you in touch with your children.

*   *   *

The years that a woman subtracts from her age are not lost. They are added to the ages of other women.

*   *   *

Still, if nobody dropped out at the eighth grade, who would hire the college graduates?

*   *   *

To find out a girl's faults, praise her to her girlfriends.

* * *

Women's styles may change, but their designs remain the same.

* * *

If a politician tries to buy votes with private money, he is a dirty crook; but if he tries to buy them with the people's own money, he's a great liberal.

* * *

Many a child who watches television for hours will go down in history, not to mention arithmetic, English, and geography.

* * *

People seldom think alike until it comes to buying wedding presents.

* * *

A halo has only to fall 11 inches to become a noose.

* * *

A man's horse sense deserts him when he is feeling his oats.

* * *

Confucius say, ostrich who keep head in sand too long during hot part of day gets burned in end.

*   *   *

He charged nothing for his preaching, and it was worth every penny of it.

*   *   *

What this country needs is a good five-cent nickel.

*   *   *

The worst thing about history is that every time it repeats itself, the price goes up.

*   *   *

No man needs a vacation as much as the person who just had one.

*   *   *

I do most of my work sitting down; that is where I shine.

*   *   *

Running into debt doesn't bother me, it's running into my creditors that's upsetting.

*   *   *

Many of our ambitions are nipped in the budget.

QUIET

A patient in a mental hospital placed his ear to the wall of his room, listening intently.

"Quiet," he whispered to an orderly and pointed to the wall.

The attendant pressed his ear against the wall, listened, and then said, "I don't hear anything."

"I know," replied the patient, "it's awful; it's been this way for days."

QUITTING

"My boss was sorry when I told him I was quitting next week."

"He was probably hoping it was this week."

RABBIT'S FOOT

First husband: I carry a rabbit's foot in my pocket because it saves me lots of money.

Second husband: How is that?

First Husband: Every time my wife sticks her hand in my pocket she thinks it's a mouse.

RAGMAN

Wife: There's an old-clothes man at the door.

Husband: Tell him I've got all the clothes I need.

RANSOM

Kidnapper: Lady, we are going to hold you until your husband ransoms you.

Woman: Oh, dear. I wish now that I had treated William a little better.

REALISM

Artist: This is my latest painting. It is called Builders at Work. It is a piece of realism.

Customer: But, I don't see any of the men at work.

Artist: Of course not—that is the realism part of it.

RECOVERY

On August 7, 1990, the old gentleman suffered a stroke, but with the loving care of his family and his kind and efficient nurse, he never fully recovered.

REDEMPTION

A man wanted to arrange for the disposal of a $5000 bond, so he called his bank.

"Sir," said the clerk, "is the bond for redemption or conversion?"

After a long pause, the man said, "Well, am I talking to the First National Bank or the First Baptist Church?"

REFERENCE

Letter of reference: This employee has worked for me for one week and I am satisfied.

RELIEF

Tom: Every time I pass a girl she sighs.

Jerry: With relief.

RENT

Pete: How much are they asking for your apartment rent now?

Jeff: About twice a day.

REPORTER

A brand-new reporter was sent out by the editor to cover the story of a man who could sing opera without interruption, while he was eating a seven-course meal.

The reporter came back and did not write-up the story.

The editor wanted to know the details.

"Oh, there was not much to it. The guy had two heads."

RESPONSIBLE

Employer: We want a responsible man for this job.

Applicant: Well, I guess I'm your man. In all the other jobs I have worked at, whenever anything went wrong, they told me I was responsible.

REST

"My uncle was finally put to rest last week."

"I didn't know that he had passed away."

"He didn't, but my aunt did."

RESORT

An Indian from a reservation in Arizona was visiting Washington, D.C. While wandering around the town, he was stopped by a native of the city who asked, "How do you like our town?"

"All right," said the Indian. "And how do you like our country?"

RIGHT

Boss: What do you mean by arguing with that customer? Don't you know our rule? The customer is always right.

Employee: I know it But he insisted that he was wrong.

ROMEO AND JULIET

Man: I'm sorry I can't come to your party tonight. I have an engagement to see Romeo and Juliet.

Woman: That's all right. Bring them along, too.

ROUND

Ruth: Where did Walter go?

Juliet: He's 'round in front.

Ruth: I know what he looks like, I just wanted to know where he went.

RUBBER BAND

Kathy: Did anyone around here lose a roll of bills with a rubber band?

Stan: Yes, I did.

Kathy: Well, I've found the rubber band.

RULE

First husband: Do you agree with the prediction that women will be ruling the world in the year 2000?

Second husband: Yes, they will still be at it.

RUN

Recent studies reveal that city-dwellers do not walk for their health . . . they run.

RUSSIA

First Russian prisoner: What are you in for?

Second prisoner: I came to work late. How about you?

First prisoner: I came to work early, so they arrested me on suspicion.

Third prisoner: Well, I'm here because I arrived at work exactly on time.

Second prisoner: What kind of offense is that?

Third prisoner: They said I must own an American watch.

SAFETY

As the pastor of a local church entered the pulpit he was handed a note to be read to the congregation. The note said, "Mark Anderson having gone to sea, his wife desires the prayers of the congregation for his safety."

The pastor picked up the slip and read aloud, "Mark Anderson having just gone to see his wife, desires the prayers of the congregation for his safety."

SALARY

"I understand his salary goes to five figures."
"Yeah—a wife and four children."

SALESMAN

Sales manager: Did you get any orders today?
Salesman: Yes, I got two orders.
Sales manager: What for?
Salesman: One to get out and the other to stay out.

SANTA CLAUS

Mother: Well, Lisa, did you see Santa Claus last night?
Lisa: No. It was too dark to see him, but I heard what he said when he stubbed his toe against the chair in the living room.

*   *   *

Elmer: Mother, where did all these pretty toys come from?

Mother: Why, dear, Santa brought them.

Elmer: Did he bring everything? Did he bring the electric train, the baseball glove, the ice skates...?

Mother: Yes, he brought everything.

Elmer: Well, who buys all the things in the stores?

SAXOPHONE

"Would you donate five dollars to bury a saxophone player?"

"Here's 30 dollars, bury six of them."

SCANDAL

Bill: Have you heard the latest scandal?

Tom: No, my wife's out of town.

SCHOOL DAZE

Father: Did you learn the three R's at college?

Son: You bet. Rah! Rah! Rah!

* * *

Teacher: If you cut an apple into 4 pieces it is called quarters. And if you slice it into 8 pieces it is called eighths. What is it called when you slice it into 8000 parts?

Student: Applesauce.

* * *

Teacher: How much is six and four?
Student: That's about eleven, ain't it?
Teacher: Six and four are ten.
Student: Six and four couldn't be ten, because five and five are ten.

*   *   *

Father: What did you learn in school today, Clarence?
Clarence: How to whisper without moving my lips.

*   *   *

Teacher: If I laid four eggs over there, and four eggs over here, how many eggs would I have?
Student: I don't think you can do it, teacher.

*   *   *

First father: What's your boy going to be when he finishes college?
Second father: An octogenarian.

*   *   *

President of the college: Are you a student here?
Student: No, I just go to college here.

*   *   *

Father: My son was a four-letter man in college.
Friend: Really?
Father: Yeah, D-U-M-B.

*   *   *

Joe: What was your college yell?
Moe: Lend me five bucks.

* * *

According to statistics, last year over 23-million American families paid a lot of money for things that looked funny and didn't work. Three million of these were antiques, the rest were college students.

* * *

Teacher: What comes after "G"?
Student: Whiz.
Teacher: No. Let's try again. What comes after "T"?
Student: "V".
Teacher: No. I'll give you just one more chance. What comes after "O"?
Student: Boy!

* * *

Teacher: Why don't you write more clearly?
Student: Then you'll realize that I can't spell.

* * *

Neighbor: When do you like school best?
Little girl: When it's closed.

* * *

Teacher: How do you spell puma?

Student: P-O-O-M-A.

Teacher: The dictionary spells it P-U-M-A.

Student: You didn't ask me how the dictionary spells it. You asked me how I spell it.

*   *   *

Boy: I got a hundred in school today.

Father: That's great! What did you get a hundred in?

Boy: Two things. I got 50 in spelling and 50 in arithmetic.

*   *   *

Mother: I think our son is going to be an astronaut.

Father: What makes you think so?

Mother: I spoke to his teacher today. She said he is taking up space.

*   *   *

Father: How did you do on your tests today?

Son: I did what Abraham Lincoln did.

Father: What was that?

Son: I went down in history.

*   *   *

"I don't think we'll do too bad," said the student to the professor, referring to an upcoming football game.

The professor chided him for his bad grammar, pointing out that he should have said badly.

"Oh," said the student, "what difference does an 'ly' make?"

"Well," said the professor, "suppose you see a girl coming down the street. It makes a difference whether you look at her stern, or sternly."

*　　*　　*

Today we spend $60,000 for a school bus to pick up the kids right at the door so they don't have to walk. Then we spend over a million dollars for a gym so the kids can get some exercise.

*　　*　　*

Teacher: Name the four seasons.
Student: Pepper, salt, vinegar, and mustard.

*　　*　　*

Student: I'm very tired. I was up till midnight doing my homework.
Teacher: What time did you begin?
Student: Eleven fifty-five.

*　　*　　*

Father: I hope you're not talking in class anymore!
Son: Not anymore...just about the same amount.

SCOTCHMAN

A Scotchman fell down a well. The water was way over his head and icy cold, but he could swim. He kept himself afloat and called out until his wife came to the edge of the well.

"I can't do a thing," she called down. "Just try to keep your head up and I'll call the men in from the field to pull you out."

"What time is it?"

"A little before 11 o'clock," she said.

"Well, don't ring for the boys now. Let them work until lunch time. I'll swim around till then."

*   *   *

Did you hear about the Scotchman who counted his money in front of the mirror so he wouldn't cheat himself?

*   *   *

Clerk: Sir, there's a Scotchman at the counter who wants to buy 10 cents worth of poison to commit suicide. Is there something I can do to save him?

Store owner: Tell him it will cost 20 cents.

SEA GULL

Becky: Look at my new baby brother. The stork brought him.

Max: He looks more like a sea gull dropped him.

SECRET

Keeping a secret from my wife is like trying to sneak the dawn past a rooster.

SEEDS

Farmer: Is this seed guaranteed?

Merchant: It certainly is. If the seed doesn't grow, just bring it back, and we'll refund the money.

SHELLFISH

Q. Where do shellfish go to borrow money?

A. To the prawnbroker.

SHORT STORY

Harry: I'm putting everything I know into my next story.

Carry: I get it—a short story.

SIGNS OF THE TIMES

FREE! FREE!

One shoe shined absolutely free.

*　　*　　*

On the desk of a kindergarten teacher:

THINK SMALL

*　　*　　*

Pawnshop sign:

PLEASE SEE ME AT YOUR
EARLIEST INCONVENIENCE.

*　　*　　*

Sign in office:

THE EASIEST WAY TO MAKE ENDS MEET
IS TO GET OFF YOUR OWN.

* * *

Sign at butcher shop:

HONEST SCALES—
NO TWO WEIGHS ABOUT IT.

* * *

Sign by stuffed fish on the wall:

IF I HAD KEPT MY MOUTH SHUT
I WOULDN'T BE HERE.

* * *

Sign on travel agency window.

PLEASE GO AWAY!

* * *

Sign in undertaker's window:

DRIVE CAREFULLY—WE CAN WAIT.

* * *

Sign at cafe:

EAT HERE AND YOU'LL NEVER
EAT ANYPLACE ELSE AGAIN!

* * *

Sign on bankrupt store:
OPENED BY MISTAKE.

*   *   *

Sign in a reducing-salon window:
WE CAN TAKE YOUR BREADTH AWAY.

*   *   *

Misprint on sign at drug store:
YOU CAN BE SURE OF HAVING
YOUR PRESCRIPTIONS FILLED
WITH SCARE AND KILL.

*   *   *

Sign in laundry window:
WE DO NOT TEAR YOUR LAUNDRY
WITH MACHINERY, WE DO IT BY HAND.

*   *   *

Sign in restaurant:
IF YOU ARE OVER 80
AND ACCOMPANIED BY YOUR PARENTS,
WE WILL CASH YOUR CHECK.

SILENCE

Husband: I haven't done anything. I have sat here and listened to you in silence, for more than an hour.

*   *   *

When someone complained to Calvin Coolidge about his habitual silence he replied, "Well, I found out early in life that you didn't have to explain something you hadn't said."

SING

Son: Why is father singing to the baby so much tonight?
Mother: He is trying to sing her to sleep.
Son: Well, if I were her, I'd pretend I was asleep.

SINGING

Kathy: My husband is just the opposite of me. While I sing he grumbles and growls.
Nancy: Then why don't you stop singing?

*   *   *

"I spent over $100,000 on voice lessons, learning to sing."
"I would love for you to meet my brother."
"Is he a singer, too?"
"No, he's a lawyer. He might be able to get your money back."

*   *   *

Judge: It seems to me that I have met you before.
Man: You have, Your Honor. I gave your daughter singing lessons.
Judge: Thirty years.

SMART

A salesclerk asked his boss how to handle women who complained about the current prices compared to the low prices in the good old days.

"Just act surprised and tell them you didn't think that they were old enough to remember them."

SMILE

The bus was very crowded . . . the highway was very busy . . . and the road was snow-covered. A woman passenger persisted in asking the driver if he had come to her stop yet.

Finally she asked, "How will I know when we get to my stop?"

The driver said, "By the big smile on my face, lady."

SMOGARIA

The country of Smogaria is a neutral country. Smogarians are about as dumb as they come. They really need help! In fact, their library only has one book in it, their national bird is the fly, and in their last beauty pageant, nobody won. When asked how many Smogarians it takes to screw in a light bulb, they responded, "What's a light bulb?"

*　　*　　*

The Smogarians are such a curiosity that a whole book may someday be dedicated to them. If you have met some Smogarians, you might want to write down your experience and send it to Smogarians, P.O. Box 9363, Fresno, California 93792. Listed below are some the latest run-ins with Smogarians.

Q. How do Smogarian fishermen count the daily catch of fish?
A. One fish...two fish...another fish...another fish...another fish....

* * *

Q. What do you call a Smogarian with half a brain?
A. Gifted.

* * *

Q. What is the smallest building in Smogaria?
A. The Hall of Fame.

* * *

Q. Why are Smogarian mothers so strong?
A. It comes from raising dumbbells.

* * *

Q. What do you have when you extend the first finger of your right hand?
A. A Smogarian handkerchief.

* * *

Q. What is gross stupidity?
A. One hundred, forty-four Smogarians.

*　　*　　*

Q. What does it say on the bottom of Coke bottles in Smogaria?
A. Open the other end.

*　　*　　*

Q. How much does a Smogarian pay for a haircut?
A. Four dollars—a dollar for each side.

*　　*　　*

Q. How do you make a Smogarian shish kebab?
A. Shoot an arrow into a garbage can.

*　　*　　*

Q. Why do Smogarians have scratched faces on Monday morning?
A. Because they eat with knives and forks over the weekend.

*　　*　　*

Q. What do they call a group of Smogarian paratroopers?
A. Air pollution.

*　　*　　*

Q. How did the employer of a large company know that he had hired a Smogarian secretary?
A. There was white-out all over the computer screen.

*　　*　　*

Q. Why did the Smogarian big-game hunter give up hunting for elephants?
A. He got tired carrying around the decoys.

*　　*　　*

Q. What happened to the Smogarian when he learned that he had been promoted from second grade to third grade?
A. He was so excited that he cut himself while shaving.

*　　*　　*

Q. What do you call a Smogarian who practices birth control?
A. A humanitarian.

*　　*　　*

Q. What do you call an attractive woman in Smogaria?
A. A tourist.

*　　*　　*

Q. Why were the Smogarians so excited when a new bridge was built across one of their widest rivers?

A. Because they could swim across the river in the shade.

* * *

Q. Why do Smogarians drink less Kool-Aid than other folks?
A. Because they have such a hard time getting two quarts of water into those little envelopes.

* * *

Did you hear about the Smogarian who thought that radioactivity was an exercise program on the radio?

* * *

Did you hear about the two Smogarians who were building a house? One of them kept throwing away half of the nails.
"What's the matter?" said the other Smogarian.
"About half of these nails have the head on the wrong end."
"You fool," said the other Smogarian. "Those are for the other side of the house."

* * *

Did you hear about the two Smogarians who committed a bank robbery? As they sped down the road one of the Smogarians said, "Look behind us and see if the cops are following us."
"How will I know?" said the other Smogarian.

"They will have their flashing red lights on."
"Do you see any of the police following us?"
"Yes ... No ... Yes ... No ... Yes ... No ...
Yes ... No ... Yes ...."

*   *   *

Teacher: What shape is the earth?
Smogarian: I dunno.
Teacher: Well, what kind of earrings does your girl-friend wear?
Smogarian: Square ones.
Teacher: No, I mean the ones she wears on Sunday.
Smogarian: Round.
Teacher: Then, what shape is the earth?
Smogarian: Square on weekdays and round on Sun-days.

*   *   *

Did you hear about the two Smogarians who were hunting in the woods? Before long, they realized that they were lost and could not get back to civilization.
"Don't worry," one of them said. "When you're lost in the woods, all you have to do is fire three shots in the air."
They did so and waited. An hour later they did it again, and still no one came. Finally they tried a third time.
"This had better work," the other Smogarian said. "These are our last arrows."

*   *   *

Did you hear about the Smogarian who went to the store for some birdseed?

"For which kind of bird?" asked the clerk.

"Oh, I dunno," replied the Smogarian. "Whichever kind will grow the fastest."

*   *   *

Three men were sitting around a table at a restaurant discussing the strides mankind has made in the 20th century.

"If you ask me," said the first man, "the smartest invention of our time is the computer. Think of all the figuring and word processing it can do with just the press of a button."

The second man said, "The computer is great, but it is not as complicated as the cruise missile. Imagine being able to follow a target wherever it goes."

Shaking his head, the third man, a Smogarian, said, "You're both way off base. The smartest invention of the 20th century is the thermos."

The other two men looked at him and said in unison, "The thermos?"

"You bet. It keeps hot things hot, and cold things cold. Now tell me: How does it know?"

*   *   *

During the war, an Englishman, a Frenchman, and a Smogarian were captured by the Germans. Each man was sentenced to stand before a firing squad.

The Englishman was the first to be put against the wall. Standing back, the German said, "Ready, aim . . ."

At which point the Englishman shouted, "Earthquake!"

The firing squad ran for cover, and the Englishman escaped.

Regrouping, the Germans put the Frenchman against the wall. Once again the German said, "Ready, aim..."

"Flood!" the Frenchman yelled.

Once again the Germans panicked, and the prisoner escaped.

Finally, the Smogarian faced the guns. But he was ready to use the same tactic that the Englishman and the Frenchman used.

The German said, "Ready, aim..."

"Fire!" hollered the Smogarian.

SMOKING

First smoker: I see that you smoke the same kind of cigarettes that I do.

Second smoker: Yes, but I don't save the coupons on the back. Do you?

First smoker: Of course. How do you think I got my artificial lung!

SNORING

Patient: Doctor, you've got to do something to help me! I snore so loudly that I keep waking myself up.

Doctor: In that case, sleep in another room.

SNOWFLAKE

Mankind should learn a lesson from the snowflake. No two of them are alike, and yet observe how well they cooperate on major projects, such as tying up traffic.

SOAP

First lady: Just look at this. I have managed to entirely furnish one of the rooms in our house by collecting soap coupons.

Second lady: Aren't you going to furnish the other six rooms?

First lady: I can't. They're full of soap.

SOBER

The first mate on a ship got drunk for the first time in his life. The ship's captain, a stern and rigid man, recorded in his log, "The first mate got drunk today."

The mate protested against the entry, explaining that if it remained in the log without further comment or explanation it could ruin his career because it suggested that drunkenness was not unusual for him, whereas he had never been drunk before. The captain, however, was adamant, stating that the log recorded the exact truth and therefore must stand as written.

The next week it was the mate's turn to write the ship's log. And on each day he wrote, "The Captain was sober today."

SORRY

Warden: I'm sorry. I find that we have kept you here a week too long.

Convict: That's all right, sir. Knock it off the next time.

SOUP

Rich: What are you eating?
Dave: Calves' brains and oxtail soup.
Rich: That's one way of making ends meet.

SPAGHETTI

Patient: You see, Doctor, I have this habit of collecting spaghetti. My entire living room is filled with it.
Psychiatrist: Why don't you put it in the closet?
Patient: There's no room. That's where I keep the meatballs.

SPINACH

Mother: Robbie, eat your spinach. It's good for growing children.
Robbie: Who wants to grow children?

SPINSTER

First spinster: Why did you sell your double bed and buy twin beds?
Second spinster: Because every night I look under the bed to see if a man is there. With two beds, my chances are doubled.

SPEECH

"He made an unusually good after-dinner speech."

"What did he say?" "He said, 'Waiter, give me the check.'"

SPECTACLES

Wife: What are spectacles?

Husband: Spectacles are glasses that people look through.

Wife: If you looked through a window would you call it a spectacle?

Husband: It depends on what you saw.

SPELLING

First boy: I couldn't learn to spell.

Second boy: Why not?

First boy: My teacher always changes the words.

SPOUTING OFF

Be reminded of the whale: When it's spouting off, that is when it is in the most danger of being harpooned.

SQUEAKS

Wife: George, wake up, there's a mouse in the bedroom. I can hear it squeaking.

Husband (as he rolled over): What do you want me to do? Get up and oil it?

SQUIRREL

Wife: You don't expect me to wear this old squirrel

coat the rest of my life do you?

Husband: Why not? The squirrels do!

STATISTICS

Statistics prove that marriage is a preventive of suicide. But, on the other hand, they also prove that suicide is a preventive of marriage.

STEADY

Worker: I'm a steady worker.

Boss: You sure are. If you were any steadier, you would be motionless.

STINK

Coach (to referee): You stink!

Referee (who picked up the football, marked off another 15 yard penalty, and turned to the coach): How do I smell from here?

STOP THE PRESSES

The following are misprints in signs, newspapers, or church bulletins:

Mr. Carlson won a 10-pound turkey at Saturday's shurkey toot.

*　　*　　*

At the Ladies Aid Society meeting many interesting articles were raffled off. Every member brought something they no longer needed. Many members brought their husbands.

*   *   *

First printing: Mr. Janelli was a defective in the police force.
Correction: Mr. Janelli was a detective in the police farce.

*   *   *

The wildwife league will meet tonight.

*   *   *

Nine volunteers put in new church furnace.

*   *   *

Father of 10 shot—Mistaken for rabbit.

*   *   *

Dr. Jeremiah is the author of a brand-new book that is expected to outsmell the two-million copies of his first book.

*   *   *

Man found dead in cemetery.

*   *   *

For sale: A full-blooded cow, giving three gallons of milk, two tons of hay, a lot of chickens, and a cookstove.

*   *   *

The general will remain unequaled in history for his accomplishment on the bottlefield.

*   *   *

Help Wanted: Adult or mature teenager to babysit. One dollar an hour, plus frige benefits.

*   *   *

Lost: Gray and white male cat. Answers to electric can opener.

*   *   *

The church had a going away party for Pastor Hanson. The congregation was anxious to give him a little momentum.

*   *   *

Found: False teeth, in parking lot at the Walters Department Store. Please come in and smile at the switchboard operator, and she will return them to you.

*   *   *

Twenty-five-year friendship ends at altar.

* * *

Dead policeman on force 17 years.

* * *

The Army has tested some new explosives recently. In fact, they dropped four-ton blondes on the test site.

* * *

City officials talk rubbish.

* * *

Sign in window: Don't kill your wife. Let our washing machine do the dirty work.

* * *

Pastor Moore has spoken in the largest Baptist churches in America. To miss hearing him will be the chance of a lifetime!

* * *

For Sale: Two plots in lively Fairmount Cemetery.

* * *

From a church bulletin: Ushers will swat late-comers at these points in the service.

* * *

Clarksville, Tennessee, which calls itself the largest outdoor mule market in the world, held a mule parade yesterday, headed by the governor.

SAINT PETER

Heckler: I wouldn't vote for you if you were Saint Peter!

Politician: If I were Saint Peter you wouldn't be in my precinct.

STOCKS

March is a very dangerous month in which to speculate in stocks. The other months are April, May, June, July, August, September, October, November, December, January, and February.

STONES

The following are famous birthstones:
    For architects, the cornerstone.
    For beauties, the peachstone.
    For borrowers, the touchstone.
    For burglars, the keystone.
    For cooks, the puddingstone.

For editors, the grindstone.
For laundresses, the soapstone.
For motorists, the milestone.
For pedestrians, the tombstone.
For policemen, the pavingstone.
For politicians, the blarneystone.
For soldiers, the bloodstone.
For stockbrokers, the curbstone.
For tourists, the Yellowstone.

STRIKE

One particular company was having a problem with all the employees going on a sit-down strike.

A very smart executive told the strikers that they might as well be comfortable, so he provided them with blankets and cases of brandy. When the brandy was half-consumed, the boss sent in 10 young women to entertain the sit-downers. Then he brought over the strikers' wives so that they could see how comfortable their husbands were. That ended the sit-down strike.

* * *

One sit-down strike in a public building was ended very quickly. The official in charge of the building simply locked all the toilets.

* * *

"My uncle is still on strike."
"How long has he been on strike?"
"Fifty-two years."

STUDY

Why study? The more we know, the more we forget. The more we forget, the less we know. The less we know, the less we forget. The less we forget, the more we know. So why study?

SUBMARINE

First rookie: Did you volunteer for submarine service?

Second rookie: No sir. I don't want to get on a ship that sinks on purpose.

SUPERIOR

Son: Dad, do you think that the American Indians were superior to the white men who took this land from them?

Father: You bet. When the Indians were the sole occupants of this land, they had no taxes, no national debt, no centralized government, no military draft, no foreign-aid programs, no banks, no stock markets, no nuclear weapons, and their women did all the work. What could be more superior than that?

SUPPER

Mother (to manager of a movie theater): Did my little boy come in here at 12:00? He had on a blue sweater and a red cap. He has blond hair.

Manager: Yes, he is sitting in the fourth row.

Mother: Do you mind giving him this package? It's his supper.

SWEET DREAMS

Q. Why did Clarence sprinkle sugar all over his pillow?

A. He wanted to have sweet dreams.

SWEETHEART

Millionaire: What's your name, driver?

Driver: Alfred, sir.

Millionaire: I always call my drivers by their last names.

Driver: It's Sweetheart, sir.

Millionaire: Drive on, Alfred.

SYRUP

After a very long introduction, the evening speaker got up and said, "Now I know how a pancake feels when they pour syrup on it."

TANTRUM

Teenager: Can I call you back in around 15 minutes? I can't talk now, I'm in the middle of a tantrum.

TAP

Q. What is the best cure for water on the brain?

A. A tap on the head.

TAXES

There is one difference between a tax collector and a taxidermist. The taxidermist saves the skin.

* * *

First friend: Two things we're sure of—death and taxes.

Second friend: Yeah, but one thing about death, it doesn't get worse every time Congress meets.

TEA BAG

Kathy: My husband has dreadful table manners. He always holds his little pinky finger out when he holds a cup of tea.

Julie: In society it is considered polite to hold out your little pinky when drinking tea.

Kathy: With the tea bag hanging from it?

TEMPT

"Keep your feet where they belong."
"Don't tempt me."

TENNIS

A very overweight man was discussing his tennis game with a friend.

"My brain barks out commands to my body: Run forward speedily! Start right away! Hit the ball gracefully over the net! Get back into position!"

"Then what happens?" asked the friend.
"And then, my body says, 'Who, me?'"

TERMITES

Dan: What do termites do when they want to relax?
Stan: They take a coffee-table break.

TITANIC

Q. What do you get if you cross the Atlantic on the Titanic?
A. Very wet.

THINK

My wife and I always think exactly alike, only she usually has the first think.

THIRSTY

Pete: I had an operation and the doctor left a sponge in me.
Bill: Got any pain?
Pete: No, but boy do I get thirsty.

THUMB-SUCKER

A little boy was in the habit of sucking his thumb all the time. His mother tried everything to break him of the habit. Finally, one day she pointed to a fat man with a very large stomach and said that the man had grown his big stomach because he did not stop sucking his thumb.

The next day the child was with his mother in a supermarket, and he kept staring at a woman with a stomach that was obviously not at all normal, in fact she was very pregnant.

Finally the annoyed woman said to the child, "Stop staring at me like that. You don't know who I am."

"No," said the boy, "but I know what you have been doing."

THREE FEET

"I've got a brother with three feet."

"What do you mean?"

"Well, my mother got a letter from my brother and he said, 'You would hardly know me—I've grown three feet.'"

TOO LONG

The master of ceremonies got up to close the meeting after a very long-winded speaker. "You have just been listening to that famous Chinese statesman, On Too Long."

TOUGH

I don't want to say that I live in a bad neighborhood, but the criminals are so tough that they attack people with chewed-off shotguns.

TRAIN

Porter: Did you miss that train, sir?

Man: No! I didn't like the looks of it, so I chased it out of the station.

TRICKLE

Teacher: What does trickle mean?

Student one: To run slowly.

Teacher: Good. And what does anecdote mean?

Student two: It's a short, funny tale.

Teacher: Well done. Now, give me a sentence with both of those words in it.

Student three: Our dog trickled down the street wagging her anecdote.

TROUBLE

Professor: Name a product in which the supply always exceeds the demand.

Student: Trouble.

*　　*　　*

If you help a man who is in trouble, he'll never forget you—especially the next time he gets into trouble.

TRUTH

Pompous politician: I was never whipped but once in my life, and that was for telling the truth.

Heckler: It sure cured you, didn't it?

UNDERTAKER

"This letter from your father indicates he's an undertaker."

"Yes, that's right."

"But you said he was a doctor."

"Oh, no. You must have misunderstood. I said that he followed the medical profession."

UNLUCKY

Kenny: I think we had better get going Friday.

Lenny: Not Friday. That's an unlucky day.

Kenny: I was born on Friday, and I don't think it's unlucky.

Lenny: Yeah, but what do your parents think?

VICE PRESIDENT

A man who had just been promoted to vice president boasted of it so much to his wife that she finally said, "Vice presidents are a dime a dozen. Why, in the supermarket they even have a vice president of prunes!"

Furious, the husband phoned the supermarket with the expectation of refuting his wife. He asked to speak to the vice president in charge of prunes.

"Which one?" was the reply. "Packaged or bulk prunes?"

WAITER..., OH WAITER!

Customer: Waiter! There's a fly in my soup!

Waiter: Don't worry sir, the spider in the bread will get it.

*   *   *

Customer: Waiter! There's a fly in my soup!
Waiter: Don't worry! The frog will surface any moment now.

*   *   *

Customer: Waiter! There's a fly in my soup!
Waiter: Okay, here's a flyswatter.

*   *   *

Customer: Waiter! There's a fly in my soup!
Waiter: Just a moment, sir—I'll get some fly spray.

*   *   *

Customer: Waiter! There's a fly in my soup!
Waiter: Now there's a fly that knows good soup.

*   *   *

Customer: Waiter! There's a fly in my soup!
Waiter: Go ahead and eat him, there's more where he came from.

*   *   *

Customer: Waiter! There's a fly in my soup!
Waiter: Just wait until you see the main course.

*   *   *

Customer: Waiter! There's a fly in my soup!
Waiter: Yes sir, better sip it with care.

*   *   *

Customer: Waiter! There's a fly in my soup!
Waiter: Serves the chef right. I told him not to strain the broth through the flyswatter.

*   *   *

Customer: Waiter! There's a fly in my soup!
Waiter: That's funny. There were two of them when I left the kitchen.

*   *   *

Customer: Waiter! There's a fly in my soup!
Waiter: Half a fly would be worse.

*   *   *

Customer: Waiter! There's a fly in my soup!
Waiter: Shhhhhhh! Everyone will want one.

*   *   *

Customer: Waiter! There's a fly in my soup!
Waiter: It can't be, sir. You're eating a noon lunch... and this is a fly-by-night place.

*   *   *

Customer: Waiter! What's this fly doing in my soup?

Waiter: Dunno, sir. It looks like the backstroke to me.

* * *

Customer: Waiter! There's a dead fly swimming in my soup!

Waiter: Nonsense, sir. Dead flies can't swim.

* * *

Customer: Waiter! There's a fly in my applesauce!

Waiter: Of course, sir. It's a fruit fly.

* * *

Customer: Waiter! What's this cockroach doing in my soup?

Waiter: We ran out of flies.

* * *

Customer: Waiter! There's a twig in my soup!

Waiter: Sorry, sir. I'll go get the branch manager.

* * *

Customer: Waiter! I can't seem to find any oysters in this oyster soup.

Waiter: Would you expect to find angels in angel food cake?

* * *

Customer: Waiter! I'm so hungry I could eat a horse!

Waiter: You certainly came to the right place.

* * *

Customer: Waiter! I'll have some kidleys.

Waiter: Do you mean kidneys, sir?

Customer: That's what I said, didle I?

* * *

Customer: Waiter! This sausage has meat at one end and bread at the other.

Waiter: Well, sir, you know how hard it is to make both ends meet these days.

* * *

Customer: No, I won't have any mushrooms, waiter. I was nearly poisoned by them last week.

Waiter: Is that so? Then I've won my bet with the cook!

* * *

Customer: Waiter! This food is terrible. I won't eat it! You had better get the manager.

Waiter: Won't do any good, mister. The manager wouldn't eat it either.

* * *

Waiter: Would you like your coffee black?
Customer: What other colors do you have?

* * *

Customer: Is your water supply healthy?
Waiter: Yes, sir. We only use well water.

* * *

Customer: Waiter! This coffee tastes like soil.
Waiter: Yes, sir, it was ground this morning.

* * *

Waiter: May I help you with the soup, sir?
Customer: What do you mean, help me? I don't need any help.
Waiter: Sorry, sir. From the sounds, I thought you might want to be dragged ashore.

* * *

Customer: Waiter! There's no chicken in my chicken soup!
Waiter: There's no horse in the horseradish, either.

WALL STREET

"I hear that your uncle lost his wealth on Wall Street."

"Yes, that is true. He was standing on the corner and dropped his last quarter into the sewer."

WART

Willy: They tell me that the way to get rid of a wart is to bury a cat. Do you think that will work?

Billy: Yes, if the wart is on the cat.

WARTS

A man walked into a doctor's office with a frog growing out of his ear.

Doctor: When did you first notice it?

Frog: It started with a wart.

WEATHER GAUGE

A tourist stopped at a country gas station. While his car was being serviced, he noticed an old-timer basking in the sun with a piece of rope in his hand. The tourist walked up to the old-timer and asked, "What do you have there?"

"That's a weather gauge, sonny," the old-timer replied.

"How can you possibly tell the weather with a piece of rope?"

"It's simple," said the old-timer. "When it swings back and forth, it's windy. And when it gets wet, it's raining."

WEDDING

Christy: Do you think it's unlucky to postpone a wedding?

Lisa: Not if you keep on doing it.

* * *

"It's a dollar and sense wedding."
"What do you mean?"
"He hasn't a dollar and she hasn't any sense."

WELL-DEVELOPED

Lucy: What well-developed arms you have.
Betty: Yes, I play a lot of tennis.
Lucy: You ride horseback, too, don't you?

WHAT'S THE DIFFERENCE?

"Take 2345 from 3769. What's the difference?"
"That's what I say, What's the difference?"

WHEELBARROWS

One day a fellow started through the gate of a large factory wheeling a wheelbarrow full of sawdust and was stopped by the guard. He told the guard he had permission to take the sawdust out of the factory.

The guard checked and found out that this was correct, and so he let the fellow go on his way. This same thing continued for many days thereafter.

Finally, a fellow worker asked the sawdust collector what he was up to. "Are you stealing all this sawdust, or what?"

"No," was the reply, "not sawdust—I'm stealing wheelbarrows."

WHISPER

Some people believe everything you tell them... especially if you whisper it.

WHISTLE

Mark: I'll bet you're one of those people that drop their work and beat it as soon as the 5:00 P.M. whistle blows.

Clark: Not me. After I quit work I usually wait about 10 minutes for the whistle to blow.

WIFE

A husband was reading a newspaper when he came across the following ad:

> What we want is a night watchman who will watch, alert and ready for the slightest noise or indication of a burglar. Somebody who can sleep with one eye and both ears open and is not afraid to tackle anything.

Husband: Honey, I think I have found the job you are looking for.

WINDY

Two farmers were boasting about the strongest wind they'd seen.

"In California," said one, "I've seen the fiercest wind in my life. You know those giant redwood trees? Well, the wind once got so strong, that it bent them right over."

"That's nothing," said the other. "Back on my farm in Iowa, we had a terrible wind one day that blew a hundred miles per hour. It was so bad, one of my hens had her back turned to the wind and she laid the same egg six times."

WISH

Husband: Why do you always wish for something you haven't got?

Wife: What else could one wish for?

WORK

The following announcement was placed on the bulletin board of a large company:

To all employees: Because of increased competition and a keen desire to remain in business, we find it necessary to institute a new policy. Effective immediately, we are asking that somewhere between starting and quitting time—without infringing too much on the time devoted to lunch period, coffee breaks, rest periods, story-telling, ticket-selling, golfing, auto racing, vacation planning, and rehashing of yesterday's TV programs—that each employee try to find some time that can be set aside and be known as *The Work Break*.

* * *

The only time people work like a horse is when the boss rides them.

* * *

First man: Why do you wear dark glasses?
Second man: Because I can't bear to see my wife work so hard.

*   *   *

Dan: I'm so nearsighted that I nearly worked myself to death.
Stan: What does being nearsighted have to do with working yourself to death?
Dan: I couldn't tell whether the boss was watching me or not, so I had to work all the time.

*   *   *

First man: Why don't you work? Hard work never killed anyone.
Second man: You're wrong. I lost both of my wives that way.

*   *   *

First man: It's no disgrace to work.
Second man: That's what I tell my wife.

WORSE

I took her for better or worse—but she's much worse than I took her for.

WRITER

Writer: Have you read my latest joke book?
Friend: No, I only read for pleasure or profit.

*   *   *

Writer: Have you read my latest joke book?
Friend: Not yet. But I shall lose no time reading it.

* * *

Writer: Have you read my latest joke book?
Friend: No. But I have no doubt that your joke book will fill a much-needed void.

* * *

Writer: Just think ... my parents didn't want me to become a well-known author.
Friend: I guess they got their wish.

INDEX

About the Author

BOB PHILLIPS...is the author of over 30 books with combined sales of over 3,000,000 copies in print. He is a licensed marriage, family, and child counselor in California. Bob received his bachelor's degree from Biola University, master's degree from Cal State University in Fresno, and his Ph.D. in counseling from Trinity Seminary. He is presently the Executive Director of Hume Lake Christian Camps, one of America's largest youth and adult camping programs.

If you would like to receive a descriptive flyer with a full description of Bob's books, along with prices, please send a self-addressed stamped envelope to:

FAMILY SERVICES
P.O. Box 9363
Fresno, CA 93702